Collins

11+
Practice
Papers

Book 2
4 complete sets of tests

Philip McMahon

About this Book

The 11+ tests

In most cases, the 11+ selection tests are set by GL Assessment (NFER), CEM or the individual school. You should be able to find out which tests your child will be taking on the website of the school they are applying to or from the local authority.

These practice test papers are designed to reflect the style of the CEM tests, but provide useful practice and preparation for all 11+ tests and common entrance exams.

Collins also publishes other practice test papers for both the CEM and the GL Assessment tests.

The CEM 11+ tests

The CEM exam consists of two papers and in each paper pupils are tested on their abilities in verbal, non-verbal and numerical reasoning. Exams are separated into small, timed sections delivered by audio instructions.

It appears the content required for CEM exams changes from year to year, and the level at which pupils are tested ranges from county to county. This book helps your child to practise working under timed conditions, recognise their strengths and weaknesses and improve their exam technique.

Contents

Inside you will find:
- Eight test papers
- An answer sheet for each test paper
- A complete set of answers with explanations
- Notes for parents, including instructions on how to complete and mark each test paper
- Tips to support 11+ preparation

You can download free audio from our website to practise answering questions under realistic exam conditions.

How to use these papers

Contained within this book are eight 45-minute test papers, as well as separate, predominantly multiple-choice answer sheets that simulate the exam environment. There are also audio instructions to download and listen to during each mock exam at **collins.co.uk/11plus**.

For more detailed information on how to best use the test papers, please see the 'Guidance for Parents' on page 3.

Further answer sheets can be downloaded from our website: **collins.co.uk/11plus**

The importance of practice

Practice will help your child to do his or her best on the day of the tests. Working through a number of practice tests allows your child to practise answering a range of test-style questions. It also provides an opportunity to learn how to manage time effectively, so that time is not wasted during the test and any 'extra' time is used constructively for checking.

Get better results

- Use these papers to help your child get used to answering questions under time constraints.
- Help your child gain confidence in their abilities.
- Use the test scores to identify areas where further practice is needed.
- Help your child revise and practise problem areas.
- Talk about coping with pressure.
- Let your child know that tests are just one part of school life.
- Let them know that doing their best is what matters.
- Plan a fun incentive for after the 11+ tests, such as a day out.

ACKNOWLEDGEMENTS

The author and publisher are grateful to the copyright holders for permission to use quoted materials and images.

Every effort has been made to trace copyright holders and obtain their permission for the use of copyright material. The author and publisher will gladly receive information enabling them to rectify any error or omission in subsequent editions. All facts are correct at time of going to press.

Published by Collins
An imprint of HarperCollins*Publishers*
1 London Bridge Street
London SE1 9GF

HarperCollins*Publishers*
1st Floor, Watermarque Building,
Ringsend Road, Dublin 4, Ireland

ISBN 9780008483951

First published 2021

10 9 8 7 6 5 4 3 2 1

© HarperCollins*Publishers* Ltd 2021

British Library Cataloguing in Publication Data.

A CIP record of this book is available from the British Library.

Publishers: Sundus Pasha and Clare Souza
Author: Philip McMahon
Project Manager: Richard Toms
Reviewing: Maravandio Ltd (trading as The Sensible Tuition Company)
Typesetting and artwork: Jouve India Private Limited
Cover Design: Kevin Robbins and Sarah Duxbury
Printed in the UK by Martins the Printers

Please note that Collins is not associated with CEM in any way. This book does not contain any official questions and it is not endorsed by CEM.

Our question types are based on those set by CEM, but we cannot guarantee that your child's actual 11+ exam will contain the same question types or format as this book.

Contents

Test A Paper 1	**5**
Test A Paper 2	**27**
Test B Paper 1	**48**
Test B Paper 2	**69**
Test C Paper 1	**87**
Test C Paper 2	**111**
Test D Paper 1	**132**
Test D Paper 2	**153**
Answers	**175**
Answer sheets	**193**

Guidance notes for parents

What your child will need to sit these papers

- A quiet place to sit the exam
- A clock which is visible to your child
- A way to play the audio download
- A pencil and an eraser
- A piece of paper

Your child should not use a calculator for any of these papers.

How to invigilate the test papers

Your child should sit Test A, Paper 1 then have a 15-minute break. They should then sit Paper 2. Don't help your child or allow any talking. Review the answers with your child and help improve their weaker areas. At later dates, your child should sit Test B, Test C and Test D in separate two-hour sessions for each.

Step 1: Remove the answers and keep them hidden from your child.

Step 2: Remove the answer sheet section. Your child should write their full name on top of the first answer sheet. Give them the question paper booklet. They must not open the paper until they are told to do so by the audio instructions.

Step 3: Start the audio.

Step 4: Ask your child to work through the practice questions before the time starts for each section. An example is already marked on each section of the answer sheet. Your child should mark the answer sheet clearly and check that the practice questions are correctly marked.

Step 5: Mark the answer sheet. Then, together with your child, work through the questions that were answered incorrectly. When working through the Non-Verbal Reasoning sections, ensure you have the question papers open to help explain the answers to your child.

How your child should complete the answer sheet

Your child MUST NOT write their answers on the question paper; they must use the answer sheet. They should put a horizontal line through the boxes on the answer sheet. To change an answer, your child should fully erase the incorrect answer and then clearly select a new answer. Any rough workings should be done on a separate piece of paper.

The audio instructions

All papers have audio instructions to allow your child to learn, listen and act upon audio instructions.

Audio instructions are at the start, during and at the end of the sections. Audio warnings on the time remaining will be given at varying intervals. Your child should listen out for these warnings.

The symbols at the foot of the page

Written instructions are at the foot of the page. Your child MUST follow these instructions:

Continue working   Stop and wait for instructions

Your child can review questions within the allocated time, but must not move onto the next section until they are allowed to do so.

The instructions and examples at the beginning of the section

In the instructions, your child should look for: the time allowed; how many questions there are; and how to complete the answers.

Examples are at the beginning of every section to show the type of question included in a particular section. The example questions will be worked through as part of the audio instructions.

Developing time-management skills and working at speed

These test papers have been used with previous pupils of the CEM exam in various counties. They provide essential practice of the types of questions which could arise, in addition to the strictly timed conditions, which will help your child practise their time-management skills.

Marking and scores

Each question is worth one mark. Overall scores your child should be aiming for:

- 75% or more on Test A and Test C if taken in the weeks leading up to the exam
- 70% or more on Test B and Test D if taken in the weeks leading up to the exam.

A weighted score attaches a certain amount of weight to each section in the exam.

How to work out your child's score:

Add together the scores obtained in both papers of a particular test for Non-Verbal Reasoning and Maths sections (both Numeracy and Problem Solving). This will give you score A.

Then add together the remaining scores for all English sections, which will give you score B.

Then add scores A and B together and divide them by 2.

This will give you an average weighted score across the two papers.

To calculate your child's weighted score as a percentage, divide your child's score by the maximum score, and multiply it by 100.

Once you have completed this, you will have two percentages and the combined weighted score across the two papers is the middle of these two percentages.

For example: If your child scores 24 out of 48 for English on the first paper of Test B, this equals 50%. If they score 28 out of 35 for English on the second paper of Test B, this is 80%. So the combined score across the two papers is 50% + 80%, which equals 130%. If you divide this by 2, this equals 65%. This is your child's weighted score.

The maximum scores are:

	Test A, Paper 1	Test A, Paper 2	Test B, Paper 1	Test B, Paper 2	Test C, Paper 1	Test C, Paper 2	Test D, Paper 1	Test D, Paper 2
English	49	43	48	35	39	57	34	57
English (per test)	92		83		96		91	
Maths and NVR	36	43	37	41	52	25	43	25
Maths and NVR (per test)	79		78		77		68	

Please note: As the content varies from year to year in CEM tests, a good score on these papers does not guarantee a pass, and a lower score may not always suggest a fail!

What happens if your child does not score a good mark?

Continue to provide a wide variety of questions to build your child's knowledge. Focus on the areas in which your child did not perform as well.

Allow your child to continue practising working under timed conditions.

Test A Paper 1

Instructions

1. Ensure you have pencils and an eraser with you.

2. Make sure you are able to see a clock or watch.

3. Write your name on the answer sheet.

4. Do not open the question booklet until you are told to do so by the audio instructions.

5. Listen carefully to the audio instructions given.

6. Mark your answers on the answer sheet only.

7. All workings must be completed on a separate piece of paper.

8. You should not use a calculator, dictionary or thesaurus at any point in this paper.

9. Move through the papers as quickly as possible and with care.

10. Follow the instructions at the foot of each page.

11. You should mark your answers with a horizontal strike, as shown on the answer sheet.

12. If you want to change your answer, ensure that you rub out your first answer and that your second answer is clearly more visible.

13. You can go back and review any questions that are within the section you are working on only. You must await further instructions before moving onto another section.

Symbols and Phrases used in the Tests

 Instructions    Time allowed for this section    Stop and wait for further instructions    Continue working

Comprehension

INSTRUCTIONS

 YOU HAVE 9 MINUTES TO COMPLETE THE FOLLOWING SECTION.

YOU HAVE 10 QUESTIONS TO COMPLETE WITHIN THE TIME GIVEN.

EXAMPLES

Comprehension Example

Some people choose to start their Christmas shopping early in October. It has been reported that some people even buy their Christmas presents in the sales in August. In recent years, people have had the option of purchasing their Christmas presents online.

Example 1

According to the passage, what is the earliest that people start their Christmas shopping?

A   In the preceding summer
B   In the preceding October
C   In the preceding November
D   Christmas Eve
E   In early December

The correct answer is A. This has already been marked in Example 1 in the Comprehension section of your answer sheet.

Practice Question 1

In recent years, what has caused a change in how people shop?

A   There are more shops.
B   Shops are more crowded.
C   You can easily organise your journey to the shops.
D   New products are available.
E   There has been a rise in use of the Internet.

The correct answer is E. Please mark this in Practice Question 1 in the Comprehension section of your answer sheet.

STOP AND WAIT FOR FURTHER INSTRUCTIONS

Read the following passage and then answer the questions below.

The Storm

Like many others my age, I had been sent away from the war-torn city to the relative safety of the countryside. According to my parents, the fighting would soon be over and we would be reunited in no time at all. Mrs Allerton, my mother's sister, had offered to take me in for the duration of the war, claiming that an educated boy like myself would be a good influence on her son Billy. I had been made to feel very welcome at Barberry Hall, I had my own room and Billy had kindly offered me a share of his toys. Being four years older than Billy, I had grown out of toys but I hadn't the heart to tell him, so I accepted them graciously. It was the third day of my stay and I arose feeling tired, my sleep disturbed by a terrible storm. Having never experienced a storm like it, I assumed that storms in the countryside must be far worse than in the city. In any case, I had by now grown accustomed to sleepless nights; visions of explosions and sounds of screaming often plagued my dreams. I dressed quickly and made my way down to breakfast, it was still early so I couldn't yet smell the familiar odour of bacon and eggs. Billy was seated at the table and Mrs Allerton was busying herself in the kitchen, singing as she worked.

"Edward, did you hear the storm last night?" shouted Billy excitedly when he saw me enter the room. I was about to say that I had been kept awake all night by the unrelenting crashes of thunder, but Mrs Allerton had at this point noticed my presence and suddenly exclaimed how wonderful it was to see me awake so early. She went on to question me on my breakfast choices, and by the time I had been seated and fed, the subject of the storm had been skilfully avoided by my aunt.

After breakfast, we hurriedly completed our morning chores and as soon as possible we ventured outside to see if there were any signs of the storm. A light mist covered the garden making it difficult to see clearly, and an eerie silence filled the air, not even a bird uttered a sound. Billy was the first to notice that the old oak tree with the newly built tree house had disappeared, in fact it had completely vanished without a trace! It was then that we noticed it wasn't just the oak tree that had gone: the shed, the fence and even the neighbours' houses were no longer there! As we looked around it became evident that there wasn't a house in sight. By this time Billy and I were starting to feel uneasy, unable to make sense of what we had seen, or more to the point, not seen. We were tempted to run back inside and pretend everything might return to normal, but we were gripped by an urge to explore and find out where everything had gone. Almost at the same time, we raced to where the old oak tree once stood and searched for traces of debris. It was difficult to see through the mist, but even after a thorough search we found nothing, absolutely nothing but grass and bare soil.

Suddenly Mrs Allerton's voice came booming through the back door, telling us to tidy the bedrooms properly. Unwilling to share our secret, and fearing we might not be allowed to explore further if an alarmed Mrs Allerton were to declare the garden unsafe, we reluctantly postponed our adventure and returned to the house. Tidying, and then having the tidied rooms checked, felt like it would take forever, but amazingly, before long we were allowed to resume our quest. As we ran out of the house we heard faint warnings of wind and rain, so to avoid further interruptions we took waterproofs and boots. By now the mist was starting to clear so we ventured farther from the house, first in one direction, then the other. Each time we were met with emptiness. Where the garden ended there was now just grass. The view into the distance was still obscured by an ominously persistent mist. I went in search of the driveway,

CONTINUE WORKING

but it was no longer there and it now seemed impossible to leave the garden. The farther we went, the denser the mist became and we were eventually forced to turn back.

"Don't worry, once the mist has lifted we'll be able to see beyond the garden again," I mumbled to Billy, but even I didn't really believe that. It didn't explain why everything apart from Barberry Hall had seemingly vanished without a trace. Then it came to me, a far more sinister thought that I couldn't share with Billy. Maybe there was nothing beyond the garden. Maybe it wasn't the neighbours that had disappeared in the storm.

(1) Why has Edward been sent away from home?

A	He has been sent to the city during the war
B	He has been sent to the countryside because it is a healthier place to live
C	He has been sent to his aunt's house to teach Billy
D	He has been sent to the countryside to fight in the war
E	He has been evacuated from the city because of the war

(2) Why was Mrs Allerton keen for Edward to stay at Barberry Hall?

A	She was very fond of her nephews
B	She needed some help around the house
C	She considered him a good role model for Billy
D	She had never met her nephew and was excited at the prospect of meeting him
E	She hoped it would encourage her sister to stay at Barberry Hall

(3) Why hadn't Edward told Billy he didn't want to play with his toys?

A	Billy forced him to take the toys
B	Billy had been kind; Edward didn't want to hurt Billy's feelings
C	The toys reminded him of home
D	He was heartless and didn't want Billy to have the toys
E	He spoke a different language and didn't know how to tell Billy

(4) What had disturbed Edward's slumber the night before?

A	Dogs barking
B	The smell of bacon and eggs
C	The sound of fighting
D	A storm
E	Mr and Mrs Allerton arguing

(5) What had happened to the old oak tree?

A	It had disappeared
B	It had grown too big and had been cut back by the gardener
C	It had been cut down to make way for a tree house
D	It had blown down in the storm and was lying on the grass
E	It had been made into a tree house

CONTINUE WORKING

6 In the context of the passage, what type of word is 'eerie'? (paragraph 3)

    A   Preposition
    B   Abstract noun
    C   Verb
    D   Pronoun
    E   Adjective

7 What had delayed the boys' adventure in the garden?

    A   Heavy rain
    B   Their daily household jobs
    C   A visit from the neighbours
    D   Mrs Allerton had declared the garden unsafe
    E   Edward needed to pack for his journey home

8 In the context of the passage, what is the meaning of 'postponed'? (paragraph 4)

    A   Increased the pace
    B   Abandoned, never to be completed
    C   Started with immediate effect
    D   Delayed until later
    E   Continued

9 Why didn't the boys tell an adult what they had seen outside?

    A   They were afraid they wouldn't be allowed to continue exploring the garden
    B   They couldn't find Mr or Mrs Allerton
    C   The Allertons were busy, they didn't want to disturb them
    D   They were too frightened to talk
    E   They were about to tell the Allertons but forgot because they were enjoying themselves too much

10 Using the text, select the option which best answers the following question:

What did the boys do to avoid being called back to the house a second time?

    A   They took their coats and boots in case it rained
    B   They took a packed lunch
    C   They took a mobile telephone and promised to call every hour
    D   They left the Allertons a note and a map of where they were going
    E   They finished their homework

STOP AND WAIT FOR FURTHER INSTRUCTIONS

Shuffled Sentences

INSTRUCTIONS

 YOU HAVE 8 MINUTES TO COMPLETE THE FOLLOWING SECTION.

YOU HAVE 15 QUESTIONS TO COMPLETE WITHIN THE TIME GIVEN.

EXAMPLES

Example 1

The following sentence is shuffled and also contains one unnecessary word. Rearrange the sentence correctly in order to identify the unnecessary word.

dog the ran fetch the to stick gluing.

A	B	C	D	E
gluing	dog	ran	the	stick

The correct answer is A. This has already been marked in Example 1 in the Shuffled Sentences section of your answer sheet.

Practice Question 1

The following sentence is shuffled and also contains one unnecessary word. Rearrange the sentence correctly in order to identify the unnecessary word.

pushed Emma stood up and closed the table under the chairs.

A	B	C	D	E
chairs	stood	under	closed	Emma

The correct answer is D. Please mark this in Practice Question 1 in the Shuffled Sentences section of your answer sheet.

STOP AND WAIT FOR FURTHER INSTRUCTIONS

Each sentence below is shuffled and also contains one unnecessary word.
Rearrange each sentence correctly in order to identify the unnecessary word.

1. needed a licence for her driving fame photograph she

A	B	C	D	E
fame	photograph	needed	licence	for

2. there dispersed a depart of wind and strong leaves was the gust

A	B	C	D	E
wind	depart	leaves	gust	dispersed

3. room by reminded aware the sign to midday vacate their guests

A	B	C	D	E
midday	room	vacate	sign	aware

4. receive a loyalty all customers with a accrued card will discount

A	B	C	D	E
card	accrued	will	receive	discount

5. sea the children take in their and shoes removed the paddled

A	B	C	D	E
shoes	removed	paddled	take	children

6. retreated into rabbit the excavation the rustled as the undergrowth bushes

A	B	C	D	E
bushes	rabbit	excavation	retreated	undergrowth

7. to applaud for waited start audience patiently the the show

A	B	C	D	E
applaud	waited	start	audience	for

CONTINUE WORKING

8 dragon the could defeat the bravely he although fought not sheath knight

A	B	C	D	E
fought	dragon	knight	not	sheath

9 battle scar wounded in been the seriously soldier had the

A	B	C	D	E
soldier	wounded	battle	scar	in

10 accused had after been a gruelling found trial the guilty enhance

A	B	C	D	E
after	enhance	had	guilty	found

11 meddle had been with the not advised he to inhibit equipment

A	B	C	D	E
inhibit	advised	he	equipment	with

12 over the evil end will prevail they're in good

A	B	C	D	E
in	end	good	will	they're

13 floor from her the hands smashed glass the entirety and on fell

A	B	C	D	E
glass	from	fell	entirety	smashed

14 a name of behaviour sold the puppies before was given none being

A	B	C	D	E
behaviour	none	puppies	name	sold

15 off in the cat resemble the dog pursuit of ran

A	B	C	D	E
dog	resemble	pursuit	cat	of

STOP AND WAIT FOR FURTHER INSTRUCTIONS ✖

Numeracy

 YOU HAVE 6 MINUTES TO COMPLETE THE FOLLOWING SECTION.

YOU HAVE 13 QUESTIONS TO COMPLETE WITHIN THE TIME GIVEN.

EXAMPLES

The questions within this section are not multiple choice. Write the answer to each question on the answer sheet by selecting the correct digits from the columns provided.

Example 1

Calculate 14 + 23

The correct answer is 37. This has already been marked in Example 1 in the Numeracy section of your answer sheet.

Practice Question 1

Calculate 83 – 75

The correct answer is 8. Please mark this in Practice Question 1 in the Numeracy section of your answer sheet. Note that a single-digit answer should be marked with a 0 in the left-hand column, so mark 08 on your answer sheet.

STOP AND WAIT FOR FURTHER INSTRUCTIONS

(1) What is the highest common factor of 12 and 18?

(2) Three eggs are needed in a recipe per person for a particular dish. At a wedding reception there are 70 guests being served this dish.

How many boxes of a dozen eggs will be needed (assuming no eggs are broken)?

(3) There are 20% fewer children at the party than expected. There are 20 children at the party.

How many were expected?

(4) How many weeks are there in 63 days?

(5) Ben is 2 years younger than Alan, who is currently half of Jenny's age.

If Ben is 7 in one year's time, how old is Jenny now?

(6) What number should replace ? to complete the sequence below?

10, 11, 22, 23, 46, 47, 94, ?

(7) What is the 11th value in the following series?

148, 141, 134, 127, 120, 113, ...

(8) A family has two large pizzas between 5 people for dinner. Each pizza is cut into 12 equally sized pieces.

If 2 people eat 4 pieces and 3 people eat 3 pieces, how many pieces remain?

(9) Today's date is March 1st.

How old will I be on April 1st next year, if I am now 12 years old and my birthday is March 26th?

(10) How many cl in 500 ml?

(11) How many vertices are there on a cuboid?

(12) Calculate: 17 + 3 × 2

(13) The lowest temperature one night was −7 degrees Celsius. The highest temperature the next day was 4 degrees Celsius.

Work out the change in temperature in degrees Celsius.

STOP AND WAIT FOR FURTHER INSTRUCTIONS

Problem Solving

 INSTRUCTIONS

 YOU HAVE 8 MINUTES TO COMPLETE THE FOLLOWING SECTION.

YOU HAVE 10 QUESTIONS TO COMPLETE WITHIN THE TIME GIVEN.

EXAMPLES

Example 1

Calculate the following:

If I buy five apples at 20p each and four bananas at 35p each, how much change will I receive if I pay with a £5 note?

A   £2.60
B   £3.40
C   £2.40
D   £3.60
E   £1.35

The correct answer is A. This has already been marked in Example 1 in the Problem Solving section of your answer sheet.

Practice Question 1

Calculate the following:

There are 17 people on a bus when it arrives at a bus stop. 11 people get on the bus, and 3 get off. How many people are then left on the bus?

A   28
B   31
C   34
D   25
E   14

The correct answer is D. Please mark this in Practice Question 1 in the Problem Solving section of your answer sheet.

STOP AND WAIT FOR FURTHER INSTRUCTIONS

Calculate the following.

(1) Jenson lives in London and is going on holiday to Florida. The flight is due to take 7 hours. It departs on time at 2 p.m. London time.

Due to bad weather the flight takes 1 hour longer than expected. Florida time is 5 hours behind London.

At what time does the flight arrive in the local Florida time?

A	9 a.m.	**B**	2 p.m.	**C**	9 p.m.
D	10 p.m.	**E**	5 p.m.		

(2) Janet cycles to work from home. The distance from home to work is 2 km.

If Janet cycles at an average speed of 8 km/h, how long does it take Janet to cycle to work from home?

A	30 minutes	**B**	15 minutes	**C**	1 hour
D	20 minutes	**E**	2 hours		

(3) A rectangular pond has a long side of 3 m and short side of 2 m. The pond is paved all the way around so that the paving forms a 1 m wide border. The paving slabs are square and each measure 1 m × 1 m.

Calculate the area covered by the paving slabs.

A	36 m²	**B**	12 m²	**C**	10 m²
D	14 m²	**E**	16 m²		

(4) What is the following fraction equivalent to in its simplest form: $\frac{15}{36}$

A	$\frac{5}{12}$	**B**	$\frac{1}{6}$	**C**	$\frac{5}{6}$
D	$\frac{5}{3}$	**E**	$\frac{1}{4}$		

(5) Sam initially borrowed £10,000 from the bank. The bank charges her interest of 4% each year on the amount that Sam borrowed.

How much interest does the bank charge if the £10,000 is repaid to the bank after 6 months?

A	£5,000	**B**	£4,000	**C**	£400
D	£200	**E**	£40		

CONTINUE WORKING ⇨

6 Which of the following numbers is all of the following: a prime number, an odd number and under 15?

A	9	**B**	17	**C**	2
D	13	**E**	12		

7 Ajay is taller than Blake, who is taller than Edward. Daniel is shorter than Blake and Colin. Colin is taller than Ajay. Edward is not as tall as Daniel.

Who is the tallest?

A	Ajay	**B**	Blake	**C**	Colin
D	Daniel	**E**	Edward		

8 The side of a square measures $t + 2$.

Which of the following expressions represents the perimeter?

A	$4t + 2$	**B**	$t + 6$	**C**	$t + 8$
D	$4(t + 2)$	**E**	$(t + 2)^2$		

9 A digger can dig a hole of 20 m³ in 2 hours.

How long will it take two diggers to dig holes that in total measure 40 m³? Assume the diggers dig at the same rate and start at the same time.

A	4 hours	**B**	8 hours	**C**	1 hour
D	$\frac{1}{2}$ hour	**E**	2 hours		

10 Jacob bought a ladder that collapses down into three equal-sized sections. The steps on the ladder are 30 cm apart and the ladder extends for 30 cm below the bottom step and above the top step. There are 10 steps on the ladder when fully extended.

How high is the ladder when collapsed down into three sections?

A	3 m 30 cm	**B**	1 m 10 cm	**C**	3 m 60 cm
D	1 m 20 cm	**E**	1 m		

STOP AND WAIT FOR FURTHER INSTRUCTIONS ⊗

Synonyms

INSTRUCTIONS

 YOU HAVE 7 MINUTES TO COMPLETE THE FOLLOWING SECTION.

YOU HAVE 24 QUESTIONS TO COMPLETE WITHIN THE TIME GIVEN.

EXAMPLES

Example 1

Select the word that is most similar in meaning to the following word:

cold

A	B	C	D	E
collect	fence	foggy	windy	chilly

The correct answer is E. This has already been marked in Example 1 in the Synonyms section of your answer sheet.

Practice Question 1

Select the word that is most similar in meaning to the following word:

start

A	B	C	D	E
cramped	begin	free	without	change

The correct answer is B. Please mark this in Practice Question 1 in the Synonyms section of your answer sheet.

STOP AND WAIT FOR FURTHER INSTRUCTIONS

For each row, select the word from the table that is most similar in meaning to the word above the table.

1 device

A	B	C	D	E
activate	gadget	converge	emphasise	dominate

2 recall

A	B	C	D	E
precedent	timetable	remember	eliminate	caller

3 intrepid

A	B	C	D	E
courageous	century	advantage	accidental	solution

4 default

A	B	C	D	E
treat	steep	flawed	usual	rare

5 anguish

A	B	C	D	E
crash	disguise	sorrow	settle	gaze

6 insightful

A	B	C	D	E
tolerate	summit	solitude	startle	perceptive

7 triumphant

A	B	C	D	E
concede	appeal	follow	celebratory	aware

8 lender

A	B	C	D	E
vision	exclude	loaner	leader	borrow

CONTINUE WORKING ⇨

9 ascertain

A	B	C	D	E
courage	baffled	deceitful	determine	introvert

10 insolent

A	B	C	D	E
rude	school	fractured	note	surface

11 vapour

A	B	C	D	E
debut	salon	moisture	neglect	porous

12 venomous

A	B	C	D	E
notorious	poisonous	legend	saunter	comfy

13 derive

A	B	C	D	E
evolve	perfect	true	validate	revolve

14 maritime

A	B	C	D	E
serve	recent	naval	hip	truant

15 odour

A	B	C	D	E
solo	smell	pleasant	factor	ominous

16 appoint

A	B	C	D	E
dream	pretend	stentorian	assign	disdain

CONTINUE WORKING ➡

17 gravitate

A	B	C	D	E
bide	fort	demolish	bristle	tend

18 excel

A	B	C	D	E
enter	lay	surpass	par	tat

19 selection

A	B	C	D	E
threat	preference	forge	dim	learn

20 housed

A	B	C	D	E
scrape	dawn	enclosed	trickle	doused

21 wield

A	B	C	D	E
hungry	brandish	lavish	dedicate	yield

22 tepid

A	B	C	D	E
intrepid	cause	lukewarm	manoeuvre	antidote

23 creative

A	B	C	D	E
factual	capability	depleted	imaginative	ardent

24 crave

A	B	C	D	E
take	yap	long	pelt	slam

STOP AND WAIT FOR FURTHER INSTRUCTIONS ✖

Non-Verbal Reasoning

 INSTRUCTIONS

 YOU HAVE 7 MINUTES TO COMPLETE THE FOLLOWING SECTION.

YOU HAVE 13 QUESTIONS TO COMPLETE WITHIN THE TIME GIVEN.

EXAMPLES

COMPLETE THE SEQUENCE Example 1

Select the picture from below that will complete the sequence in place of the ?

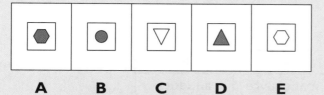

The correct answer is C. This has already been marked in Example 1 in the Non-Verbal Reasoning section of your answer sheet.

CONTINUE WORKING ⟶

COMPLETE THE SEQUENCE Practice Question 1

Select the picture from below that will complete the sequence in place of the ?

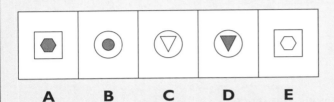

A   B   C   D   E

The correct answer is D. Please mark this in Practice Question 1 in the Non-Verbal Reasoning section of your answer sheet.

COMPLETE THE SQUARE Example 2

Which shape or pattern completes the square?

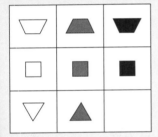
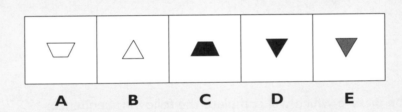

A   B   C   D   E

The correct answer is D. This has already been marked in Example 2 in the Non-Verbal Reasoning section of your answer sheet.

COMPLETE THE SQUARE Practice Question 2

Which shape or pattern completes the square?

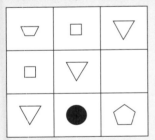
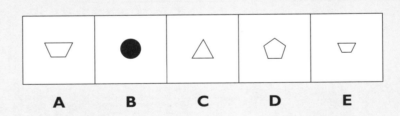

A   B   C   D   E

The correct answer is B. Please mark this in Practice Question 2 in the Non-Verbal Reasoning section of your answer sheet.

STOP AND WAIT FOR FURTHER INSTRUCTIONS ✖

1. Select the picture which will complete the following sequence:

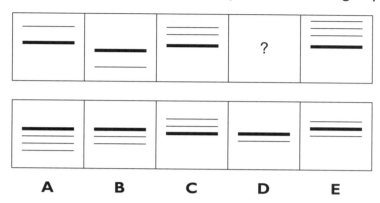

2. Select the picture which will complete the following sequence:

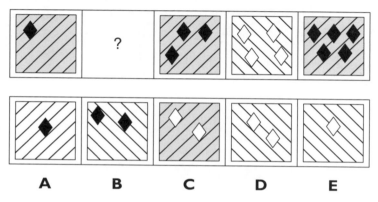

3. Select the picture which will complete the following sequence:

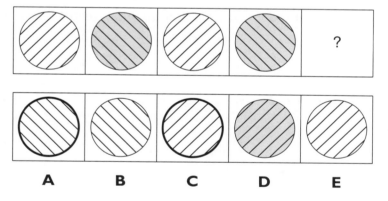

(4) Select the picture which will complete the following sequence:

A   B   C   D   E

(5) Select how this 3-dimensional image would appear when viewed from the left without rotation:

A   B   C   D   E

(6) Select how this 3-dimensional image would appear when viewed from behind:

A   B   C   D   E

(7) Select how this 3-dimensional image would appear when viewed from behind:

A   B   C   D   E

(8) Which shape or pattern completes the larger square?

A   B   C   D   E

CONTINUE WORKING ⇨

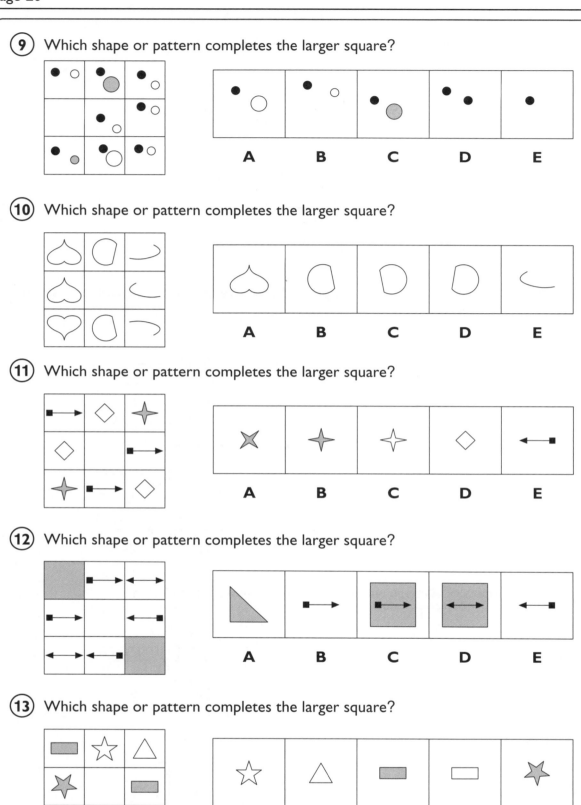

(9) Which shape or pattern completes the larger square?

A B C D E

(10) Which shape or pattern completes the larger square?

A B C D E

(11) Which shape or pattern completes the larger square?

A B C D E

(12) Which shape or pattern completes the larger square?

A B C D E

(13) Which shape or pattern completes the larger square?

A B C D E

END OF PAPER

Test A Paper 2

Instructions

1. Ensure you have pencils and an eraser with you.

2. Make sure you are able to see a clock or watch.

3. Write your name on the answer sheet.

4. Do not open the question booklet until you are told to do so by the audio instructions.

5. Listen carefully to the audio instructions given.

6. Mark your answers on the answer sheet only.

7. All workings must be completed on a separate piece of paper.

8. You should not use a calculator, dictionary or thesaurus at any point in this paper.

9. Move through the papers as quickly as possible and with care.

10. Follow the instructions at the foot of each page.

11. You should mark your answers with a horizontal strike, as shown on the answer sheet.

12. If you want to change your answer, ensure that you rub out your first answer and that your second answer is clearly more visible.

13. You can go back and review any questions that are within the section you are working on only. You must await further instructions before moving onto another section.

Symbols and Phrases used in the Tests

 Instructions  Time allowed for this section Stop and wait for further instructions Continue working

Problem Solving

 YOU HAVE 8 MINUTES TO COMPLETE THE FOLLOWING SECTION.

YOU HAVE 10 QUESTIONS TO COMPLETE WITHIN THE TIME GIVEN.

EXAMPLES

A £2.60	B £3.40	C £2.40	D £3.60	E £1.35
F 25	G 14	H 31	I 28	J 34

Example 1

Calculate the following:

If I buy five apples at 20p each, and four bananas at 35p each, how much change will I receive if I pay with a £5 note.

The correct answer is A. This has already been marked in Example 1 in the Problem Solving section of your answer sheet.

Practice Question 1

Calculate the following:

There are 17 people on a bus when it arrives at a bus stop. 11 people get on the bus, and 3 get off. How many people are then left on the bus?

The correct answer is F. Please mark this in Practice Question 1 in the Problem Solving section of your answer sheet.

STOP AND WAIT FOR FURTHER INSTRUCTIONS

Read the passage below. Several questions will then follow for you to answer. Select an answer to each question from the 10 different possible answers in the table. You may use an answer for more than one question.

A 10	B 51	C 600	D 165	E 32
F 20	G 2115	H 110	I 200	J 2045

Class 6A from Thornbury Primary School went on an end-of-year trip on 8th July. It was a trip to a theme park by coach for the day. The trip was originally planned for 18th May, but due to bad weather the theme park was closed that day.

The coach left Thornbury at 6.30 a.m. and arrived at 9.15 a.m. after travelling at an average speed of 40 mph on the journey. There were more girls than boys in the class (the ratio of girls to boys is 5 : 3). 8 adults looked after the children on the trip and they also went into the theme park.

When they arrived at the theme park, they had an offer on the ticket prices. The adult price was twice that of a child ticket price. For every adult ticket purchased, one child in the group was given free admission. The child ticket price was £15.

As they arrived slightly later than expected, all adults and children on the school trip decided to pay an additional £5 each for 'Qjump' passes to avoid the queues for rides. This applied to all, whether they had a free ticket or not.

Jack remembered that when he came last year with his parents, the child ticket price was lower than for this visit. The theme park had seen a drop in visitor numbers for the summer months of May and June due to bad weather. This year's visitor numbers were 28,056 in May and 32,784 in June. Last year, they were 31,346 for May and 36,254 for June.

The park covers an area of 2,000,000 m². The class had hoped to go on 20 of the rides. They actually managed to go on 24 as they did not spend so long in queues. The park closed at 6 p.m., and the class set off back to Thornbury on the coach at 6.30 p.m. The journey home was 30 minutes quicker as there was less traffic on the roads.

(1) How many days later than previously planned did the school trip happen?

(2) How long (in minutes) did the coach take to get to the theme park from Thornbury?

(3) There are 12 boys in class 6A. How many girls are there?

(4) What was the total cost (in £) for the adult and children tickets (excluding the 'Qjump' passes)?

(5) What was the total cost (in £) of all the 'Qjump' passes?

CONTINUE WORKING

(6) What was the percentage decrease in visitors this May and June (in total) compared to last year?

(7) How many hectares does the theme park cover?

(8) What is the percentage increase in the number of rides the class went on compared to what they had hoped for?

(9) At what time did the coach arrive back at Thornbury?

(10) How far away in miles is the theme park from Thornbury?

STOP AND WAIT FOR FURTHER INSTRUCTIONS ⬡✕

Cloze

 YOU HAVE 10 MINUTES TO COMPLETE THE FOLLOWING SECTION.

YOU HAVE 20 QUESTIONS TO COMPLETE WITHIN THE TIME GIVEN.

EXAMPLES

Example 1

Read the sentence below and select the most appropriate word from the table.

A	B	C	D	E
backdrop	carefully	drawer	disadvantage	dilution

The undulating hills were the perfect (Q1) _____ for the watercolour painting.

Please select your answer to go in the place of Q1 in the above sentence.

The correct answer is A. This has already been marked in Example 1 in the Cloze section of your answer sheet.

Practice Question 1

Read the sentence below and select the most appropriate word from the table.

A	B	C	D	E
had	interior	success	attend	absent

The girl decided she would like to (Q1) _____ the party.

Please select your answer to go in the place of Q1 in the above sentence.

The correct answer is D. Please mark the answer D in Practice Question 1 in the Cloze section of your answer sheet.

STOP AND WAIT FOR FURTHER INSTRUCTIONS

Read the passage and select the most appropriate word from the table below.

A	B	C	D	E
formerly	boarding	resembles	capacity	observation

F	G	H	I	J
capsules	revolutions	formally	prominent	intended

The London Eye

The London Eye is an (Q1) _____ wheel on the south bank of the River Thames. It was (Q2) _____ opened by the then Prime Minister Tony Blair on 31st December 1999. It was (Q3) _____ known as the Millennium Wheel and was a new landmark to commemorate the new millennium. It is the most popular paid tourist attraction with over 3 million visitors each year.

The London Eye was originally (Q4) _____ to be a temporary structure with a five-year lifetime.

The wheel has 32 sealed passenger (Q5) _____ attached to the external circumference of the wheel. Each of the 32 capsules represents one of the London boroughs. The maximum (Q6) _____ of the wheel is 800 passengers. The wheel travels slowly and does not stop to allow passengers on. The wheel moves so slowly – two (Q7) _____ per hour – that there is no need for it to stop for (Q8) _____ and disembarkation of passengers (except those with disabilities). It only travels at about 26 cm per second (approximately 1 km/h). The rim of the wheel is supported by tensioned steel cables and (Q9) _____ an enormous spoked bicycle wheel. The rim of the wheel is powered by rotating rubber tyres at the base of the structure. The wheel has a diameter of 120 m and in 2006 a decorative lighting system was installed to make it more (Q10) _____ at night.

Passengers can see spectacular panoramic views across London, particularly on a clear day as the height of the wheel is 135 m. At the time it was built, it was the tallest wheel in the world. The London Eye was the city's highest observation point before The Shard's observation deck was built. There have been over 80 million visitors since The London Eye was built. The London Eye is not the city's first big wheel: The Great Wheel was 94 metres high and opened in Earls Court in 1895 until it closed in 1906.

CONTINUE WORKING

Read the passage and select the most appropriate word from the table below.

A	B	C	D	E
distinctly	tapping	emergence	highlights	knowledgeable

F	G	H	I	J
meandered	fellow	invested	understand	appreciate

The Daily Walk

Sophie looked forward to her walk each day. It had become one of the (Q11) _____ of her day.

This was strange as she (Q12) _____ remembers loathing going for walks as a child with her family. Now that Sophie had matured, she was better able to (Q13) _____ her surroundings.

She now used all her senses; from the smell of the fresh country air (although it wasn't always that fresh!) to the views far and wide. There was very little activity where she walked, other than (Q14) _____ walkers who always greeted her cheerily. She was surprised just how much more she could hear when away from the hustle and bustle of daily life.

Sophie had become (Q15) _____ about what to look and listen out for as the seasons changed.

From the sound of the woodpecker up in the trees to the (Q16) _____ of the first shoots of snowdrops on the ground in late winter and early spring. Sophie had (Q17) _____ in a pair of binoculars to watch the woodpeckers from a distance, keen not to disturb them. She was fascinated in the way they excavated holes in tree trunks to nest, and emitted their characteristic (Q18) _____ noise as their bills drummed on the trees. It always made her day when she was lucky enough to catch a glimpse of one in action.

Should Sophie be feeling energetic, she would take the loop walk following the public footpath up through the National Trust land. She had to keep her dog Monty on a tight lead up there, since the footpath was also a bridleway. The path (Q19) _____ its way through the forest, adjacent to the undulating fields of bright yellow crop from later in spring. The sweeping views from the summit were well worth the exercise. She could (Q20) _____ why the summit had long been the site of an ancient Iron Age hill fort dating back nearly 3,000 years.

STOP AND WAIT FOR FURTHER INSTRUCTIONS ⊗

Non-Verbal Reasoning

 ## INSTRUCTIONS

 YOU HAVE 8 MINUTES TO COMPLETE THE FOLLOWING SECTION.

YOU HAVE 15 QUESTIONS TO COMPLETE WITHIN THE TIME GIVEN.

EXAMPLES

ROTATION Example 1

Select one of the images below that is a rotation of the image on the left.

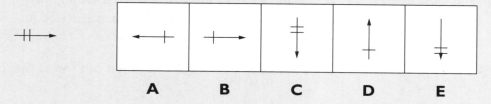

The correct answer is C. This has already been marked in Example 1 in the Non-Verbal Reasoning section of your answer sheet.

ROTATION Practice Question 1

Select one of the images below that is a rotation of the image on the left.

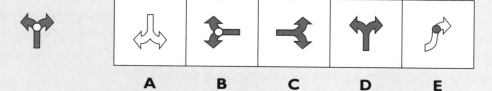

The correct answer is B. Please mark this in Practice Question 1 in the Non-Verbal Reasoning section of your answer sheet.

CONTINUE WORKING

CODES Example 2

Look at the codes for the following patterns and identify the missing code for the pattern on the far right.

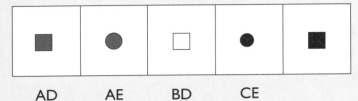

AD   AE   BD   CE

A	BE
B	AD
C	BC
D	BD
E	CD

The correct answer is E. This has already been marked in Example 2 in the Non-Verbal Reasoning section of your answer sheet.

CODES Practice Question 2

Look at the codes for the following patterns and identify the missing code for the pattern on the far right.

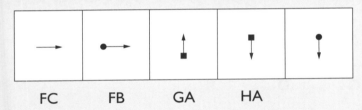

FC   FB   GA   HA

A	FA
B	GB
C	HB
D	HC
E	GC

The correct answer is C. Please mark this in Practice Question 2 in the Non-Verbal Reasoning section of your answer sheet.

STOP AND WAIT FOR FURTHER INSTRUCTIONS ⊗

1 Select one of the images below that is a rotation of the image on the left.

A B C D E

2 Select one of the images below that is a rotation of the image on the left.

A B C D E

3 Select one of the images below that is a rotation of the image on the left.

A B C D E

4 Select one of the images below that is a rotation of the image on the left.

A B C D E

5 Select one of the images below that is a rotation of the image on the left.

A B C D E

6 Select one of the images below that is a rotation of the image on the left.

A B C D E

CONTINUE WORKING

7. Select one of the images below that is a rotation of the image on the left.

A   B   C   D   E

8. Select one of the images below that is a rotation of the image on the left.

A   B   C   D   E

9. Which shape or pattern completes the larger square?

A   B   C   D   E

10. Which shape or pattern completes the larger square?

A   B   C   D   E

11. Which shape or pattern completes the larger square?

A   B   C   D   E

CONTINUE WORKING

(12) Which shape or pattern completes the larger square?

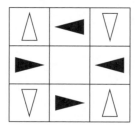
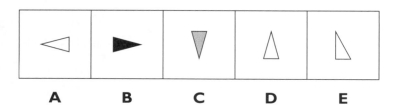

A   B   C   D   E

(13) Look at the codes for the following patterns and identify the missing code for the pattern on the far right.

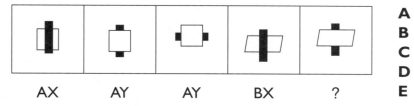

AX   AY   AY   BX   ?

A   BX
B   BY
C   AY
D   BZ
E   CY

(14) Look at the codes for the following patterns and identify the missing code for the pattern on the far right.

AE   BF   CD   BE   ?

A   AE
B   AF
C   BD
D   CD
E   GD

(15) Look at the codes for the following patterns and identify the missing code for the pattern on the far right.

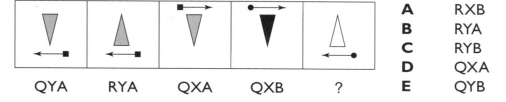

QYA   RYA   QXA   QXB   ?

A   RXB
B   RYA
C   RYB
D   QXA
E   QYB

STOP AND WAIT FOR FURTHER INSTRUCTIONS ⊗

Grammar

INSTRUCTIONS

 YOU HAVE 5 MINUTES TO COMPLETE THE FOLLOWING SECTION.

YOU HAVE 8 QUESTIONS TO COMPLETE WITHIN THE TIME GIVEN.

EXAMPLES

Example 1

Select the word below that is misspelt.

A	B	C	D	E
cinema	while	repeet	home	open

The correct answer is C. This has already been marked in Example 1 in the Grammar section of your answer sheet.

Practice Question 1

Select the correct prefix or suffix below to give the opposite to the word 'legal':

A	B	C	D	E
in	im	un	il	non

The correct answer is D. Please mark the answer D in Practice Question 1 in the Grammar section of your answer sheet.

STOP AND WAIT FOR FURTHER INSTRUCTIONS

1 Select the word below that is misspelt.

A	B	C	D	E
sentence	necessary	disappear	tomorrow	Wendesday

2 Select the word below that is misspelt.

A	B	C	D	E
chiefly	deceit	receive	adress	tranquil

3 Select the word below that is misspelt.

A	B	C	D	E
decide	desription	forever	office	pedestrian

4 Select the correct prefix to give the opposite to the word 'lead'.

A	B	C	D	E
ir	anti	mis	il	im

5 Select the correct prefix to give the opposite to the word 'logical'.

A	B	C	D	E
sub	il	re	so	int

6 Identify the word below that is an adverb.

A	B	C	D	E
rally	fly	always	between	glide

7 Identify the word below that is a preposition.

A	B	C	D	E
just	relate	almost	rejoice	throughout

8 Identify the word below that is an abstract noun.

A	B	C	D	E
luck	fortunate	against	creature	screech

STOP AND WAIT FOR FURTHER INSTRUCTIONS

Antonyms

 INSTRUCTIONS

 YOU HAVE 5 MINUTES TO COMPLETE THE FOLLOWING SECTION.

YOU HAVE 15 QUESTIONS TO COMPLETE WITHIN THE TIME GIVEN.

EXAMPLES

Example 1

Select the word that is least similar to the following word.

light

A	B	C	D	E
dark	water	feather	bright	hill

The correct answer is A. This has already been marked in Example 1 in the Antonyms section of your answer sheet.

Practice Question 1

Select the word that is least similar to the following word.

smooth

A	B	C	D	E
allow	beneath	rough	whilst	shade

The correct answer is C. Please mark the answer C in Practice Question 1 in the Antonyms section of your answer sheet.

STOP AND WAIT FOR FURTHER INSTRUCTIONS

Which word is least similar to the word above each table?

(1) justice

A	B	C	D	E
reduce	detail	rural	injustice	dedicated

(2) convinced

A	B	C	D	E
tranquillity	thoughtful	freedom	symptom	doubtful

(3) forget

A	B	C	D	E
complain	outline	amber	gesture	remember

(4) genuine

A	B	C	D	E
shatter	counterfeit	terrace	function	destination

(5) jeopardise

A	B	C	D	E
secure	construct	ember	jovial	paradise

(6) shield

A	B	C	D	E
elect	native	endanger	revenge	appeal

(7) designated

A	B	C	D	E
generated	perforated	recreated	unchartered	unspecified

CONTINUE WORKING

8 ponder

A	B	C	D	E
ace	gender	splendour	ignore	ignorance

9 summarise

A	B	C	D	E
tentative	knight	elaborate	sunrise	charming

10 entrenched

A	B	C	D	E
variable	sullen	tantalise	entertain	emblem

11 dilapidated

A	B	C	D	E
vista	strained	radiate	sturdy	serrated

12 sequential

A	B	C	D	E
dread	treacherous	random	highlight	resemble

13 wretched

A	B	C	D	E
shipwreck	cheery	fusion	mediate	reason

14 quibble

A	B	C	D	E
clique	squabble	eloquent	agree	hamper

15 extrovert

A	B	C	D	E
delectable	vertigo	withdrawn	intervene	comparable

STOP AND WAIT FOR FURTHER INSTRUCTIONS ✖

Numeracy

 YOU HAVE 9 MINUTES TO COMPLETE THE FOLLOWING SECTION.

YOU HAVE 18 QUESTIONS TO COMPLETE WITHIN THE TIME GIVEN.

EXAMPLES

Some of the questions within this section are not multiple choice. Write the answers to these questions on the answer sheet by selecting the correct digits from the columns provided.

Example 1

Calculate 14 + 23

The correct answer is 37. This has already been marked in Example 1 in the Numeracy section of your answer sheet.

Practice Question 1

Calculate 83 − 75

The correct answer is 8. Please mark the answer in Practice Question 1 in the Numeracy section of your answer sheet. Note that a single-digit answer should be marked with a 0 in the left-hand column. So mark 08 on your answer sheet.

STOP AND WAIT FOR FURTHER INSTRUCTIONS

The first 8 questions in this section are not multiple choice. For these questions you should write the answer to the question on the answer sheet by selecting the digits from the columns of brackets. For the remaining questions, select the answer A, B, C, D or E.

CONTINUE WORKING

1. Find the missing number to replace the '?' to make this equation correct:

   $6 + 4 \times ? = 2 \times 15$

2. Work out the next number in the following sequence:

   4, 7, 13, 25, 49, ?

3. There were 30 children in a class last year.

   Work out the number of children in the class this year if there are 10% fewer than last year.

4. The number of chairs in a restaurant is expressed as $4t$, where t is the number of tables.

   If there are 60 chairs, how many tables are in the restaurant?

5. There are 20 equally spaced fence posts along one side of a field. Two lengths of wire run along all the fence posts from one end to the other of the field.

   If the posts are spaced 2 metres apart, what is the total length in metres of wire used in the fence?

6. Aisha is 13 on January 1st next year. Aisha is exactly 5 years younger than Sheilesh.

   Sheilesh's mother, Mumta, is currently 34 years older than him.

   How old is Mumta now?

7. On a train at Amersham station, there are 48 passengers in carriage A, 49 passengers in carriage B and 12 passengers in carriage C.

   At the next stop, Harrow on the Hill, 12 passengers leave carriage A, 37 passengers leave carriage B, and all passengers leave carriage C. 23 new passengers board the train at this stop.

   How many passengers are on the train as it leaves Harrow on the Hill?

8. A film started at 17:25 and finished at 19:15. I only watched half of it because I fell asleep.

   How many minutes of the film did I watch?

CONTINUE WORKING

(9) Find the value of $a^2 + 1$, if $a = 5$

    A 6   **B** 26   **C** 36   **D** 11   **E** 24

(10) A total of 43 sweets are divided equally between 5 children.

How many sweets remain after they are shared out?

    A 5   **B** 8   **C** 3   **D** 4   **E** 2

(11) A supermarket opens at 8 a.m. Between opening and noon, 862 customers visit the store.

Between 3 p.m. and closing time at 9 p.m., 683 customers visit the store.

If 1,972 customers in total visited the store that day, how many came between noon and 3 p.m.?

    A 1,110   **B** 1,289   **C** 427   **D** 1,545   **E** 185

(12) There are 120 apartments in a block. 10 of them are unoccupied and empty. Of the remaining apartments, the average number of people living in each apartment is 1.8.

If the total number of people living in 109 of the occupied apartments is 195, how many people live in the one remaining occupied apartment?

    A 1   **B** 2   **C** 3   **D** 4   **E** 5

(13) How many faces are on a cuboid?

    A 8   **B** 4   **C** 6   **D** 2   **E** 9

(14) There are 26 children at a party. Each child eats a piece of birthday cake and each piece weighs 40 g.

What is the total weight of cake eaten by the children?

    A 1.04 kg   **B** 1 kg   **C** 846 g   **D** 940 g   **E** 1.4 kg

CONTINUE WORKING ⟹

(15) What is the smallest number of coins from which I could make exactly £3.42?

    A 4   **B** 7   **C** 6   **D** 5   **E** 10

(16) What is the size of the exterior angle on a regular pentagon?

    A 108°   **B** 60°   **C** 72°   **D** 90°   **E** 45°

(17) Lampposts are evenly spaced, 20 metres apart along a 2,000-metre road.

How many lampposts are there along the road?

    A 100   **B** 99   **C** 10   **D** 200   **E** 101

(18) In 3 years' time, I will be 5 years younger than my older sister, Lara.

In 4 years' time, Lara will be half of my mother's age then.

My mother is now 42.

How old am I now?

    A 56   **B** 23   **C** 17   **D** 14   **E** 11

END OF PAPER

Test B Paper 1

Instructions

1. Ensure you have pencils and an eraser with you.
2. Make sure you are able to see a clock or watch.
3. Write your name on the answer sheet.
4. Do not open the question booklet until you are told to do so by the audio instructions.
5. Listen carefully to the audio instructions given.
6. Mark your answers on the answer sheet only.
7. All workings must be completed on a separate piece of paper.
8. You should not use a calculator, dictionary or thesaurus at any point in this paper.
9. Move through the papers as quickly as possible and with care.
10. Follow the instructions at the foot of each page.
11. You should mark your answers with a horizontal strike, as shown on the answer sheet.
12. If you want to change your answer, ensure that you rub out your first answer and that your second answer is clearly more visible.
13. You can go back and review any questions that are within the section you are working on only. You must await further instructions before moving onto another section.

Symbols and Phrases used in the Tests

 Instructions  Time allowed for this section Stop and wait for further instructions Continue working

Comprehension

 YOU HAVE 8 MINUTES TO COMPLETE THE FOLLOWING SECTION.

YOU HAVE 10 QUESTIONS TO COMPLETE WITHIN THE TIME GIVEN.

EXAMPLES

Comprehension Example

Some people choose to start their Christmas shopping early in October. It has been reported that some people even buy their Christmas presents in the sales in August. In recent years, people have had the option of purchasing their Christmas presents online.

Example 1

According to the passage, what is the earliest that people start their Christmas shopping?

A   In the preceding summer
B   In the preceding October
C   In the preceding November
D   Christmas Eve
E   In early December

The correct answer is A. This has already been marked in Example 1 in the Comprehension section of your answer sheet.

Practice Question 1

In recent years, what has caused a change in how people shop?

A   There are more shops
B   Shops are more crowded
C   You can easily organise your journey to the shops
D   New products are available
E   There has been a rise in use of the Internet

The correct answer is E. Please mark this in Practice Question 1 in the Comprehension section of your answer sheet.

STOP AND WAIT FOR FURTHER INSTRUCTIONS

Read the following passage, then answer the questions below.

Blueridge Homes

We would like to inform you that we are undertaking a consultation regarding a proposal to build new homes and a landscaped area in Hampton to the south of Benson Road and west of Luckton Gate. The location is shown in the separate map, and the boundary of the proposed new site is highlighted in red.

Blueridge Homes is a market leading developer of new homes. We are committed to providing quality homes that are innovative and sustainable, with modern family at the heart of our design process. We strive to create safe and happy places for families to settle. We contribute to public amenities directly and create infrastructure to suit families' needs with respect to accessible public transport and well-maintained public green spaces that help to nourish existing wildlife and ecosystems.

Our flagship development in neighbouring Westhampton has only recently been completed and has successfully reflected our values. It was completed 2 years ago. It comprises 246 homes. Our proposed new development is named "Seaview". It is situated on slightly elevated ground from its surroundings, and consequently affords dramatic panoramic views out to the ocean (selected homes only). Seaview comprises only 60 homes, and is one of our most exclusive developments. In keeping with our values, we plan to have 24 affordable homes. Affordable homes will be a mix of 2, 3, and 4 bedroom houses. In addition, there will be a number of 5 bedroom homes. Many of the larger 4 and 5 bedroom homes are detached with south-facing gardens looking out onto the Atlantic Ocean. A computer-generated image gallery can be found at www.blueridge/seaview/gallery.com

The proposal will also include a secluded woodland area with nature trail, lake, and landscaped gardens. The existing orchard will be protected and maintained (subject to annual service charge per property). Computer-generated images can also be found in the online gallery using the website link above.

The site is currently privately owned. New road access would be made available via Benson Road. Footpath access would also be created from Luckton Gate heading west around the lake. There would also be further pedestrian access heading north through the landscaped public space towards Benson Road. Both pedestrian access options would enable residents to access local bus services. The pedestrian access from Seaview will be extended through to the established footpath connections at the popular recreational park (Lincoln Park). This will be done to provide much needed safe pedestrian routes through to the popular local primary schools. A significant financial contribution to the already agreed expansion plans at both primary schools is proposed as part of our commitment to local communities.

The site is in an Area of Outstanding Natural Beauty (AONB). All current legislation and regulations will be carefully adhered to under the supervision of the local planning authority. Indeed, we will strive to go above and beyond what is required of us under the current legislation. Our aim is to enhance what currently exists and improve the lives of not only the new residents, but the wider community too.

CONTINUE WORKING

Careful consideration has been given to how the local residents will be affected during the construction and when the new development becomes established.

Our proposals are set out in further detail by our planning consultant (Click Step Planning) and can be accessed via their website: clickstepplanning/seaview/hampton.co.uk.

We appreciate that we are planning to build in your community and we very much welcome your comments, ideas and input on how we could improve your community. Should you wish to email us, please contact:

malcolm.macintyre@clickstepplanning.co.uk

1 What is being proposed?

A More shops
B Fewer boats in the local harbour
C New school
D A new leisure centre
E New housing development

2 Where is the development situated?

A Lincoln Park
B Westhampton
C Hampton
D Atlantic Ocean
E Clickstep

3 Where is Luckton Gate in relation to the development?

A To the West
B In the development
C To the East
D Underneath
E Benson Road

4 What type of word is 'strive'?

A Adverb
B Verb
C Adjective
D Abstract noun
E Preposition

CONTINUE WORKING ⏩

5 What is the meaning of the word 'strive'?

A To be in trouble
B To really try to achieve the objective
C A group of native inhabitants established long ago
D An intricate feature of a planning map
E Occurring more than once every 2 weeks

6 What is the meaning of the word 'established'?

A Set up
B Sit down
C Well made
D Recently completed
E To be able to see through

7 What does the acronym AONB stand for?

A An Other New Build
B Alternate Occupied Neat Building
C All Out Now Begin
D Area of Outstanding Natural Beauty
E Are we On the Nature Behalf

8 In what location was the Blueridge flagship development completed two years ago?

A Westhampton
B Southampton
C Atlantic
D Lucky Gate
E Luckton Gate

9 Where could I find images of the proposed development?

A 64 Turnaround Street
B Local newspaper
C In 3 years' time when completed
D The online gallery at www.blueridge/seaview/gallery.com
E The art gallery in Westhampton

10 What is the name of the person I should contact by email to let them know my thoughts on the proposal?

A Graham Detintford
B Malcolm Macintyre
C Bluejohn and Clickstep
D Teressa Risborough
E Edward Bolton

STOP AND WAIT FOR FURTHER INSTRUCTIONS

Shuffled Sentences

INSTRUCTIONS

 YOU HAVE 10 MINUTES TO COMPLETE THE FOLLOWING SECTION.

YOU HAVE 15 QUESTIONS TO COMPLETE WITHIN THE TIME GIVEN.

EXAMPLES

Example 1

The following sentence is shuffled and also contains one unnecessary word.
Rearrange the sentence correctly, in order to identify the unnecessary word.

dog the ran fetch the to stick gluing.

A	B	C	D	E
gluing	dog	ran	the	stick

The correct answer is A. This has already been marked in Example 1 in the Shuffled Sentences section of your answer sheet.

Practice Question 1

The following sentence is shuffled and also contains one unnecessary word.
Rearrange the sentence correctly, in order to identify the unnecessary word.

pushed Emma stood up and closed the table under the chair.

A	B	C	D	E
chair	stood	under	closed	Emma

The correct answer is D. Please mark this in Practice Question 1 in the Shuffled Sentences section of your answer sheet.

STOP AND WAIT FOR FURTHER INSTRUCTIONS

Each sentence below is shuffled and also contains one unnecessary word.
Rearrange each sentence correctly, in order to identify the unnecessary word.

(1) room through the showers night will continue the

A	B	C	D	E
the	room	continue	night	though

(2) have his key through Jack forgotten may he that thought

A	B	C	D	E
through	his	may	Jack	key

(3) they choose lunch for options there were several to from

A	B	C	D	E
several	from	options	they	choose

(4) good to use the shelves were nearly filled hole and put new

A	B	C	D	E
were	use	put	shelves	hole

(5) through the dense wildflowers being careless not to woodland he weaved careful trample on the

A	B	C	D	E
dense	woodland	careless	trample	wildflowers

(6) the lane brought the countryside through country meandered

A	B	C	D	E
the	country	meandered	brought	through

(7) under the she backpack struggled over the weight of

A	B	C	D	E
she	of	over	the	backpack

CONTINUE WORKING

8 no the squid were living squalid conditions longer now appropriate

A	B	C	D	E
squid	conditions	no	appropriate	were

9 will you best city this reason summertime charming see in at its

A	B	C	D	E
this	see	city	reason	best

10 surprise the departures door at his arrival unpleasant an was

A	B	C	D	E
his	departures	door	the	surprise

11 spot the difference like this picnic looked for the perfect

A	B	C	D	E
difference	like	spot	looked	for

12 everyone was against feeling long and a been it had weary day

A	B	C	D	E
everyone	day	been	against	feeling

13 some good clock was it time had he about luck

A	B	C	D	E
was	time	had	clock	it

14 the average most popular the mode train in the city of transport had become

A	B	C	D	E
popular	had	most	of	average

15 thunder atmosphere lighting helped to create the ambient an

A	B	C	D	E
thunder	helped	atmosphere	lighting	an

STOP AND WAIT FOR FURTHER INSTRUCTIONS

Numeracy

INSTRUCTIONS

YOU HAVE 6 MINUTES TO COMPLETE THE FOLLOWING SECTION.

YOU HAVE 13 QUESTIONS TO COMPLETE WITHIN THE TIME GIVEN.

EXAMPLES

The questions within this section are not multiple choice. Write the answer to each question on the answer sheet by selecting the correct digits from the columns provided.

Example 1

Calculate 14 + 23

The correct answer is 37. This has already been marked in Example 1 in the Numeracy section of your answer sheet.

Practice Question 1

Calculate 83 − 75

The correct answer is 8. Please mark this in Practice Question 1 in the Numeracy section of your answer sheet. Note that a single-digit answer should be marked with a 0 in the left-hand column, so mark 08 on your answer sheet.

STOP AND WAIT FOR FURTHER INSTRUCTIONS

(1) Jenny's birthday is 15 days after Simon's, whose birthday is on March 18th.
On what day in April is Jenny's birthday?

(2) A pack of 52 playing cards are shared out equally among my 7 friends and myself.
How many are left over?

(3) A length of rope is sold at a price of £2.40 per metre. I would like to buy 5 m.
Calculate the cost in £.

(4) I live 20 minutes' walk from the town centre. I walk at 3 miles per hour.
How many miles is the town centre from my home?

(5) Alan is 3 years older than Barry. Barry is half of Alan's age.
How old is Barry?

(6) Find the appropriate number to replace '?' in the sequence below.
21, 20, 24, 18, ?, 16, 30

(7) What is the 21st term in the following series?
161, 154, 147, 140, 133...

(8) A cake weighs 480 g. It is cut into 8 pieces. 3 are eaten. Of the remainder, $\frac{4}{5}$ falls on the floor and is trodden on by accident. This is then disposed of.
What is the weight in grams of the remaining cake?

(9) How many quarters are there in half my age if I am 7 years old?

(10) How many cm in 350 mm?

(11) How many vertices are there on an octahedron?

(12) Calculate the following: 22 − 2 × 10

(13) Calculate the following:
The number of days in 14 weeks − The number of days in March, April and May

STOP AND WAIT FOR FURTHER INSTRUCTIONS

Problem Solving

INSTRUCTIONS

 YOU HAVE 10 MINUTES TO COMPLETE THE FOLLOWING SECTION.

YOU HAVE 10 QUESTIONS TO COMPLETE WITHIN THE TIME GIVEN.

EXAMPLES

A £2.60	B £3.40	C £2.40	D £3.60	E £1.35
F 25	G 14	H 31	I 28	J 34

Example 1

Calculate the following:

If I buy five apples at 20p each, and four bananas at 35p each, how much change will I receive if I pay with a £5 note.

The correct answer is A. This has already been marked in Example 1 in the Problem Solving section of your answer sheet.

Practice Question 1

Calculate the following:

There are 17 people on a bus when it arrives at a bus stop. 11 people get on the bus, and 3 get off. How many people are then left on the bus?

The correct answer is F. Please mark this in Practice Question 1 in the Problem Solving section of your answer sheet.

STOP AND WAIT FOR FURTHER INSTRUCTIONS

A 6	B 125	C 120	D 40	E 1,000
F 32	G 48	H 1,280	I 960	J 80

Several questions will follow for you to answer. Select an answer to each question from the 10 different possible answers in the table above. You may use an answer for more than one question.

1 Terry has a business that hires out bikes to people. He usually charges £8 per hour for adults and £4 per hour for children's bikes.

If a family of 2 adults and 2 children hire bikes for 2 hours, what is the cost in pounds?

2 A family ticket provides a family of 2 adults and 3 children with 2 hours' hire for £50.

What is the value of the discount in pounds?

3 There are a number of recommended cycle routes. The route around the lake is 12 km.

If a family cycles at an average speed of 8 km/h, and stops for 30 minutes on the route for a picnic, how long will the route take in minutes?

4 Family A sets off clockwise around the lake route at 6 km/h. Family B sets off anticlockwise on the lake route at 12 km/h.

If they set off at the same time, after how many minutes will they meet each other?

5 Terry initially borrowed £20,000 from the bank to buy the 48 bikes. The bank charges him interest of 5% each year on the amount that he borrowed.

How much interest does the bank charge each year in pounds?

6 The 48 bikes Terry bought include twice as many adult than children's bikes.

How many adult bikes were purchased by Terry?

7 On average Terry rents out each of the adult bikes for 5 hours each week. The business is closed for 12 weeks during winter.

In an average week, how much in pounds does Terry receive from renting out the adult bikes each week at £8 per hour?

8 Terry hires his premises. He pays rent to the owner each month. His rent last year was £800 per month. This year, the rent increased at the start of the year by 20%.

What is the rent each month this year in pounds?

9 Terry pays himself £12,000 per year. This is spread equally over the 12 months of the year.

How much does he pay himself each month in pounds?

10 Terry had 150 customers this year, which is a 20% increase on last year.

How many customers did Terry have last year?

STOP AND WAIT FOR FURTHER INSTRUCTIONS

Synonyms

INSTRUCTIONS

 YOU HAVE 5 MINUTES TO COMPLETE THE FOLLOWING SECTION.

YOU HAVE 23 QUESTIONS TO COMPLETE WITHIN THE TIME GIVEN.

EXAMPLES

Example 1

Select the word that is most similar in meaning to the following word:

cold

A	B	C	D	E
collect	fence	foggy	windy	chilly

The correct answer is E. This has already been marked in Example 1 in the Synonyms section of your answer sheet.

Practice Question 1

Select the word that is most similar in meaning to the following word:

start

A	B	C	D	E
cramped	begin	free	without	change

The correct answer is B. Please mark this in Practice Question 1 in the Synonyms section of your answer sheet.

STOP AND WAIT FOR FURTHER INSTRUCTIONS

Select the word from each table that is most similar in meaning to the word above the table.

1 novice

A	B	C	D	E
foible	beginner	confluence	emphatic	parched

2 impending

A	B	C	D	E
nuance	carefully	imminent	timid	depending

3 inadvertent

A	B	C	D	E
tranquil	dedicated	transcribe	accidental	absent

4 superficial

A	B	C	D	E
anguish	shallow	aspect	texture	efficacy

5 meagre

A	B	C	D	E
creature	manager	desist	compensate	scanty

6 onset

A	B	C	D	E
beginning	tease	settle	sincere	brisket

7 lapse

A	B	C	D	E
impasse	renew	slip	aspire	collapse

CONTINUE WORKING ⇨

8 obscure

A	B	C	D	E
balanced	mysterious	interior	obdurate	revolve

9 assert

A	B	C	D	E
treacherous	gesture	declare	invert	insert

10 collate

A	B	C	D	E
gather	gasp	foliage	neglect	weary

11 vouch

A	B	C	D	E
lecture	confirm	candid	decipher	assume

12 promenade

A	B	C	D	E
proactive	lemonade	liability	stroll	compete

13 ambiguity

A	B	C	D	E
languish	perpetuity	uncertainty	brevity	recall

14 maritime

A	B	C	D	E
roam	nautical	spouse	timely	tardy

15 ominous

A	B	C	D	E
luminous	venomous	sufficient	threatening	seasonal

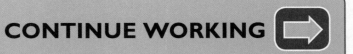

CONTINUE WORKING

16 akin

A	B	C	D	E
dreaded	proud	comparable	tussle	yacht

17 doting

A	B	C	D	E
bid	craving	devoted	brimming	indeed

18 exorbitant

A	B	C	D	E
excessive	lean	exterior	parade	absorbent

19 sever

A	B	C	D	E
thrive	weather	project	divide	lever

20 preen

A	B	C	D	E
screen	smarten	scene	babble	shift

21 orifice

A	B	C	D	E
opening	analysis	office	calamity	module

22 repudiate

A	B	C	D	E
sanctuary	reject	crevice	create	annotate

23 copious

A	B	C	D	E
fate	cope	implore	plentiful	arduous

STOP AND WAIT FOR FURTHER INSTRUCTIONS

Non-Verbal Reasoning

 INSTRUCTIONS

 YOU HAVE 6 MINUTES TO COMPLETE THE FOLLOWING SECTION.

YOU HAVE 14 QUESTIONS TO COMPLETE WITHIN THE TIME GIVEN.

EXAMPLES

COMPLETE THE SEQUENCE Example 1

Select the picture from the bottom row that will complete the sequence in place of the ? in the top row.

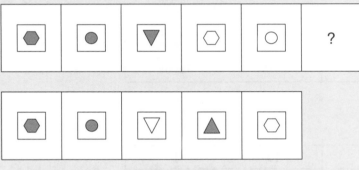

The correct answer is C. This has already been marked in Example 1 in the Non-Verbal Reasoning section of your answer sheet.

COMPLETE THE SEQUENCE Practice Question 1

Select the picture from the bottom row that will complete the sequence in place of the ? in the top row.

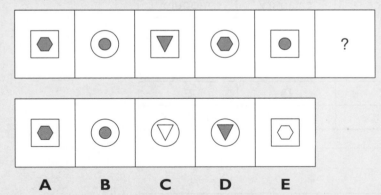

The correct answer is D. Please mark this in Practice Question 1 in the Non-Verbal Reasoning section of your answer sheet.

STOP AND WAIT FOR FURTHER INSTRUCTIONS

1 Select the picture from the bottom row that will complete the sequence in place of the ? in the top row.

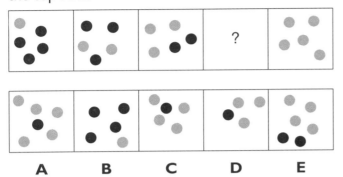

A   B   C   D   E

2 Select the picture from the bottom row that will complete the sequence in place of the ? in the top row.

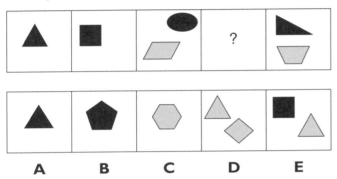

A   B   C   D   E

3 Select the picture from the bottom row that will complete the sequence in place of the ? in the top row.

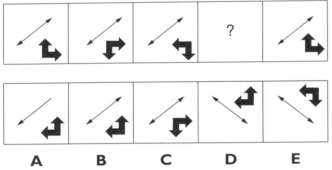

A   B   C   D   E

4 Select the picture from the bottom row that will complete the sequence in place of the ? in the top row.

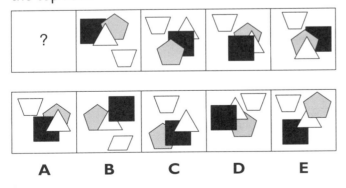

A   B   C   D   E

CONTINUE WORKING ⇨

5 Select the picture from the bottom row that will complete the sequence in place of the ? in the top row.

A   B   C   D   E

6 Select the picture from the bottom row that will complete the sequence in place of the ? in the top row.

A   B   C   D   E

7 Select the picture from the bottom row that will complete the sequence in place of the ? in the top row.

A   B   C   D   E

8 Select the picture from the bottom row that will complete the sequence in place of the ? in the top row.

A   B   C   D   E

CONTINUE WORKING ⏵

(9) Select the picture from the bottom row that will complete the sequence in place of the ? in the top row.

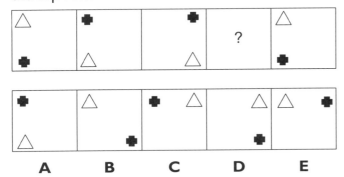

A   B   C   D   E

(10) Select the picture from the bottom row that will complete the sequence in place of the ? in the top row.

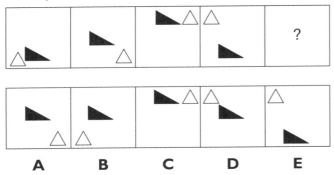

A   B   C   D   E

(11) Select the picture from the bottom row that will complete the sequence in place of the ? in the top row.

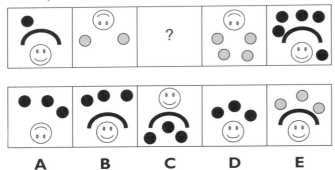

A   B   C   D   E

(12) Select the picture from the bottom row that will complete the sequence in place of the ? in the top row.

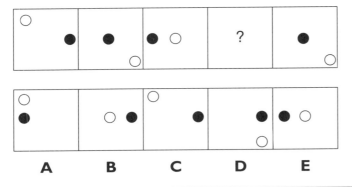

A   B   C   D   E

CONTINUE WORKING ▶

13 Select the picture from the bottom row that will complete the sequence in place of the ? in the top row.

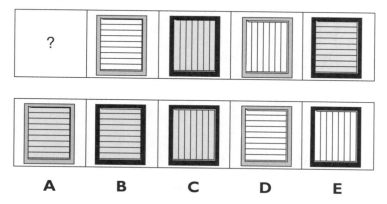

A   B   C   D   E

14 Select the picture from the bottom row that will complete the sequence in place of the ? in the top row.

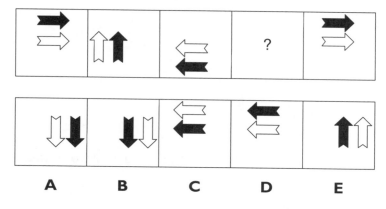

A   B   C   D   E

END OF PAPER

Test B Paper 2

Instructions

1. Ensure you have pencils and an eraser with you.

2. Make sure you are able to see a clock or watch.

3. Write your name on the answer sheet.

4. Do not open the question booklet until you are told to do so by the audio instructions.

5. Listen carefully to the audio instructions given.

6. Mark your answers on the answer sheet only.

7. All workings must be completed on a separate piece of paper.

8. You should not use a calculator, dictionary or thesaurus at any point in this paper.

9. Move through the paper as quickly as possible and with care.

10. Follow the instructions at the foot of each page.

11. You should mark your answers with a horizontal strike, as shown on the answer sheet.

12. If you want to change your answer, ensure that you rub out your first answer and that your second answer is clearly more visible.

13. You can go back and review any questions that are within the section you are working on only. You must await further instructions before moving onto another section.

Symbols and Phrases used in the Tests

 Instructions    Time allowed for this section   Stop and wait for further instructions   Continue working

Problem Solving

INSTRUCTIONS

 YOU HAVE 12 MINUTES TO COMPLETE THE FOLLOWING SECTION.

YOU HAVE 10 QUESTIONS TO COMPLETE WITHIN THE TIME GIVEN.

EXAMPLES

A	B	C	D	E	F	G	H	I	J
£2.60	£3.40	£2.40	£3.60	£1.35	25	14	31	28	34

Example 1

Calculate the following:

If I buy 5 apples at 20p each and 4 bananas at 35p each, how much change will I receive if I pay with a £5 note?

The correct answer is A. This has been marked in Example 1 in the Problem Solving section of your answer sheet.

Practice Question 1

Calculate the following:

There are 17 people on a bus when it arrives at a bus stop.
11 people get on the bus and 3 get off. How many people are then left on the bus?

The correct answer is F. Please mark the answer F in the Problem Solving section of your answer sheet.

STOP AND WAIT FOR FURTHER INSTRUCTIONS

Several questions will follow for you to answer.

A	B	C	D	E	F	G	H	I	J
75	72	68	64	53	52	70	1,500	1,600	1,084

Select an answer to each question from the 10 different possible answers in the table above.
You may use an answer for more than one question.

(1) Amelia and Josh go out for dinner. They use a voucher to get a 20% discount on the total cost of the meal.

If they save £14, what was the cost in pounds of the meal before the discount?

(2) The cost of adult tickets to the zoo is twice the price of child tickets.

If the cost of a child ticket is £10, how much in pounds will a family of 2 adults and 3 children be charged in total?

(3) There are 25% more children in a school this year compared to last year.

If there are 80 children this year, how many were there last year?

(4) Harold enjoys cycling as a hobby. He has a device on his bike that measures his top speed, average speed, distance travelled and time cycled. On his ride today, he cycled for 2.5 hours. His average speed today was 30 km/h.

How far in kilometres did Harold cycle?

(5) A new house has a trapezium-shaped rear garden that has parallel sides measuring 10 m and 6 m. The distance between the parallel sides of the garden is 8 m.

Calculate the area of the rear garden in m².

(6) The exchange rate at the time a family arranged to get some US Dollars was $1.25 (US Dollars) : £1 (British Pounds).

Excluding any transaction fee, how much did it cost the family in pounds to buy $1,875 (US Dollars)?

CONTINUE WORKING

(7) On return from their holiday, another family changed their remaining US Dollars back into British Pounds (£). The exchange rate was ($1.3 : £1). They had $91 remaining in US Dollars to exchange for British Pounds (£).

Excluding any transaction fee, how much in British Pounds (£) did they receive?

(8) A 100 m race is held at school. The fastest child runs the race in 12.604 seconds. Second place is not far behind at 12.668 seconds, and 3rd place is timed at 13.333 seconds.

How many thousandths of a second are there between 1st and 2nd place?

(9) 864 passengers boarded a cruise ship at Southampton bound for Barbados. 15 of these passengers left the ship in Florida. A further 235 passengers boarded the ship in Florida. The next stop was Barbados.

How many passengers were on the ship on arrival in Barbados?

(10) The cruise ship set sail from Southampton on June 4th. It arrived in Barbados on June 17th. It remained in Barbados for 22 days, and returned to Southampton on July 26th.

How many days (inclusive of the first and last day) was the cruise trip?

STOP AND WAIT FOR FURTHER INSTRUCTIONS ⊗

Cloze

INSTRUCTIONS

 YOU HAVE 10 MINUTES TO COMPLETE THE FOLLOWING SECTION.

YOU HAVE 20 QUESTIONS TO COMPLETE WITHIN THE TIME GIVEN.

EXAMPLES

Example 1

Read the sentence below and choose the letter next to the most appropriate word to complete it.

A backdrop	**B** carefully	**C** drawer	**D** disadvantage	**E** dilution

The undulating hills were the perfect (Q1) _____ for the watercolour painting.

Please select your answer to go in the place of Q1 in the sentence above.

The correct answer is A. This has already been marked in Example 1 in the Cloze section of your answer sheet.

Practice Question 1

Read the sentence below and choose the letter next to the most appropriate word to complete it.

A had	**B** interior	**C** success	**D** attend	**E** absent

The girl decided she would like to (Q1) _____ the party.

Please select your answer to go in the place of Q1 in the sentence above.

The correct answer is D. Please mark the answer D in Practice Question 1 in the Cloze section of your answer sheet.

STOP AND WAIT FOR FURTHER INSTRUCTIONS

Read the following passage and choose the letter next to the most appropriate word to complete each space. There are 10 questions. For example, Q1 is where you should put your answer to Question 1 on your answer sheet.

A packaging	B proud	C horrible	D willing	E looming
F environment	G reluctantly	H lethargic	I startled	J hallucinating

The Polluted Beach

There was a continual rhythmic crashing of the waves in the distance. The chilly, bitter wind, blew across Stephanie's pallid face as she stumbled over the sand dunes to get on to the beach. It was cold and wet and she was feeling particularly (Q1) _____ today so she decided to head back, but then, thinking she was (Q2) _____ , she saw a murky pile of rubbish wash up on the shore. She couldn't quite make out what it was as she squinted while the stinging water beat against her face. Battling against the wind, Stephanie headed towards it and (Q3) _____ picked a piece up.

The object looked rather like what had once been the (Q4) _____ of a rich chocolate bar. Now it was just a slimy piece of gloop. This is (Q5) _____ , she thought to herself. All of a sudden, she jumped into the air, (Q6) _____ . A burly, bearded man was (Q7) _____ over her, holding a long tool of some sort. He handed it to Stephanie. "It's a litter picker," he grunted. "I work here, keeping the beach clean." Stephanie told him that she would be (Q8) _____ to help him and so for the rest of the afternoon, that was what she did. And now, whenever she goes to the beach, she thinks of how (Q9) _____ she is of herself, for helping out on that polluted beach and for doing her part to help the (Q10) _____ .

CONTINUE WORKING ⇨

Read the following passage and choose the letter next to the most appropriate word to complete each space. There are 10 questions. For example, Q11 is where you should put your answer to Question 11 on your answer sheet.

A disgusting	**B** particular	**C** dissatisfied	**D** ornately	**E** croissants
F choose	**G** aisles	**H** toppers	**I** browsed	**J** thought

Emily's Cake-shopping Trip

Emily (Q11) _____ the shelves like there was no tomorrow! She strolled down the (Q12) _____ , looking at the rich, creamy chocolate cakes, the buttery (Q13) _____ and the deliciously iced cupcakes intricately and (Q14) _____ decorated with the most detailed cupcake (Q15) _____ she had ever seen! The biscuits and cookies looked great too but she just couldn't (Q16) _____ !

Emily then saw a fruit cake, which she (Q17) _____ looked nice, but she knew the friends who were coming to the party would find it (Q18) _____ . But then she remembered; her mum wanted her to buy a (Q19) _____ cake. Looking down at her piece of paper, she found out that it was indeed, simply a plain chocolate cake. Emily ran to the place where she saw them earlier, but they were all sold out. (Q20) _____ and disappointed, Emily reluctantly left the shop empty handed, wishing she had gone straight to that cake to get it initially.

STOP AND WAIT FOR FURTHER INSTRUCTIONS ⊗

Non-Verbal Reasoning

INSTRUCTIONS

 YOU HAVE 8 MINUTES TO COMPLETE THE FOLLOWING SECTION.

YOU HAVE 13 QUESTIONS TO COMPLETE WITHIN THE TIME GIVEN.

EXAMPLES

CUBE NET Example 1

Look at the cube net. Select the only cube that could be formed from the net.

The correct answer is E. This has already been marked in Example 1 in the Non-Verbal Reasoning section of your answer sheet.

A   B   C   D   E

CUBE NET Practice Question 1

Look at the cube net. Select the only cube that could be formed from the net.

The correct answer is A. Please mark this in Practice Question 1 in the Non-Verbal Reasoning section of your answer sheet.

A   B   C   D   E

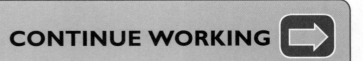

CONTINUE WORKING

LEAST SIMILAR Example 2

Select the image that is least similar to the other images.

The correct answer is B. This has already been marked in Example 2 in the Non-Verbal Reasoning section of your answer sheet.

LEAST SIMILAR Practice Question 2

Select the image that is least similar to the other images.

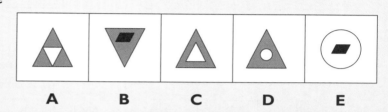

The correct answer is E. Please mark this in Practice Question 2 in the Non-Verbal Reasoning section of your answer sheet.

STOP AND WAIT FOR FURTHER INSTRUCTIONS

(1) Select the image that is least similar to the other images.

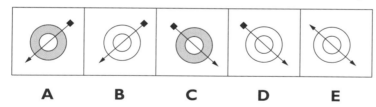

(2) Select the image that is least similar to the other images.

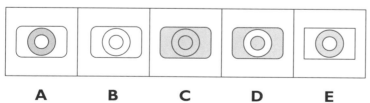

CONTINUE WORKING

(3) Select the image that is least similar to the other images.

A   **B**   **C**   **D**   **E**

(4) Select the image that is least similar to the other images.

A   **B**   **C**   **D**   **E**

(5) Select the image that is least similar to the other images.

A   **B**   **C**   **D**   **E**

(6) Select the image that is least similar to the other images.

A   **B**   **C**   **D**   **E**

(7) Look at the cube net. Select the only cube that could be formed from the net.

A   **B**   **C**   **D**   **E**

(8) Look at the cube net. Select the only cube that could be formed from the net.

A   **B**   **C**   **D**   **E**

CONTINUE WORKING ⇨

9) Look at the cube net. Select the only cube that could be formed from the net.

10) Look at the cube net. Select the only cube that could be formed from the net.

11) Look at the cube net. Select the only cube that could be formed from the net.

12) Look at the cube net. Select the only cube that could be formed from the net.

13) Look at the cube net. Select the only cube that could be formed from the net.

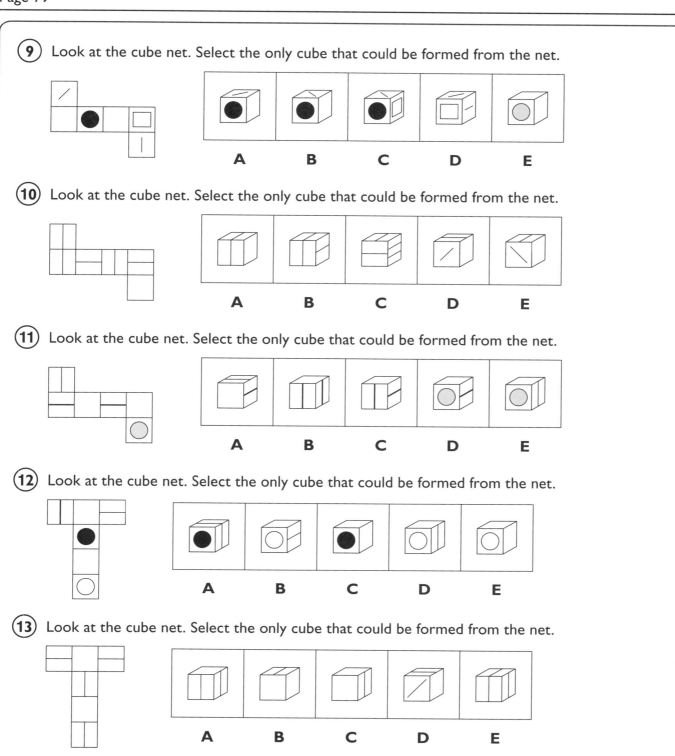

A   B   C   D   E

STOP AND WAIT FOR FURTHER INSTRUCTIONS ⊗

Antonyms

 YOU HAVE 5 MINUTES TO COMPLETE THE FOLLOWING SECTION.

YOU HAVE 15 QUESTIONS TO COMPLETE WITHIN THE TIME GIVEN.

EXAMPLES

Example 1

Select the word that is least similar to the following word:

light

A	B	C	D	E
dark	water	feather	bright	hill

The correct answer is A. This has already been marked in Example 1 in the Antonyms section of your answer sheet.

Practice Question 1

Select the word that is least similar to the following word:

smooth

A	B	C	D	E
allow	beneath	rough	whilst	shade

The correct answer is C. Please mark the answer C in Practice Question 1 in the Antonyms section of your answer sheet.

STOP AND WAIT FOR FURTHER INSTRUCTIONS

In each row, select the word from the table that is least similar to the word above the table.

(1) melancholy

A	B	C	D	E
fruity	united	incompatible	cheery	deceitful

(2) tranquility

A	B	C	D	E
peacefulness	designated	apprehension	forthright	calmness

(3) repetition

A	B	C	D	E
retort	sow	haughty	competition	infrequency

(4) detract

A	B	C	D	E
dedicate	enhance	subtract	foul	diminish

(5) espy

A	B	C	D	E
spot	detect	embrace	overlook	disorder

(6) shun

A	B	C	D	E
welcome	refute	vision	claim	construct

CONTINUE WORKING ⮞

7 destiny

A	B	C	D	E
incline	preference	recline	rigidity	valour

8 alacrity

A	B	C	D	E
acidity	jocularity	reluctance	possess	painstaking

9 renowned

A	B	C	D	E
probable	known	inane	anonymous	enchanted

10 pitiful

A	B	C	D	E
brash	substantial	tingling	vein	energetic

11 dilapidated

A	B	C	D	E
vision	sound	extrovert	decided	great

12 frank

A	B	C	D	E
intent	desperate	dishonest	sudden	remarkable

CONTINUE WORKING

(13) tedious

A	B	C	D	E
preceding	quibble	laughable	medical	interesting

(14) neglectful

A	B	C	D	E
attentive	squeamish	tactile	forgetful	heed

(15) brief

A	B	C	D	E
district	lengthy	vegetarian	detail	comfort

STOP AND WAIT FOR FURTHER INSTRUCTIONS ⊗

Numeracy

 YOU HAVE 10 MINUTES TO COMPLETE THE FOLLOWING SECTION.

YOU HAVE 18 QUESTIONS TO COMPLETE WITHIN THE TIME GIVEN.

EXAMPLES

The questions within this section are not multiple-choice. Write the answer to each question on the answer sheet by selecting the correct digits from the columns provided.

Example 1

Calculate 14 + 23

The correct answer is 37. This has already been marked in Example 1 in the Numeracy section of your answer sheet.

Practice Question 1

Calculate 83 – 75

The correct answer is 8. Write the answer in Practice Question 1 in the Numeracy section of the answer sheet. Note that a single-digit answer should be marked with a 0 in the left-hand column, so mark 08 on your answer sheet.

STOP AND WAIT FOR FURTHER INSTRUCTIONS

(1) Calculate the total number of minutes in 2 hours less the total number of days in 12 weeks.

(2) Find the missing number to replace the ? below to make the equation correct:

$2 + 3 \times ? = 4 \times 5$

(3) Calculate the next number in the following sequence:

1, 2, 4, 7, 11, ?

(4) What is the number if 18 is 2 more than 8 times this number?

For questions 5 and 6 look at the Venn diagram (right), which shows information on children in a class.

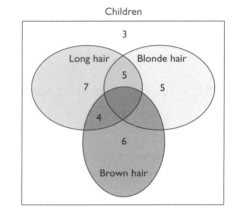

(5) How many of the children had long hair, that was not brown hair?

(6) How many children in the class did not have blonde hair?

(7) If the ratio of boys to girls in a class of 27 children is 5 : 4, how many girls are in the class?

(8) If my brother is now twice as old as I was a year ago, how old is my brother now if I am 9?

(9) As I work at the local supermarket, I receive a discount of 25% on everything I buy from there.

If I paid £60 for my weekly shopping from that supermarket, what was the original price in £ of my shopping?

(10) Find the value of a if:

$40 - a = 3a$

CONTINUE WORKING ⬛➡

(11) How many days are there from May 26th to July 15th inclusive?

(12) If 42 cards are divided equally amongst my 6 friends and myself, how many cards does each have?

(13) There are 2 whole birthday cakes at a party with 30 people attending in total. The cakes are cut so that there is exactly one piece for everyone.

If five-sixths of the cakes were eaten, how many pieces of cake remain?

(14) Bob has twice as many sweets as Jack. Jack has 3 times as many as Jan. There are 50 sweets in total.

How many does Bob have?

(15) What is the smallest number of coins from which I could make £1.76 exactly?

(16) The lowest temperature on the night of February 1st/2nd was −8 degrees Celsius. The highest temperature on March 17th was 21 degrees Celsius.

By how many degrees Celsius had the temperature risen between these two dates?

(17) Lampposts are evenly spaced 50 m apart along a 1,000 m road.

How many lampposts are there?

(18) In 2 years' time, I will be 4 years younger than my older cousin, Lucy. In 4 years' time, Lucy will be half of my mother's age then. My mother is now 40.

How old am I now?

END OF PAPER

Test C Paper 1

Instructions

1. Ensure you have pencils and an eraser with you.
2. Make sure you are able to see a clock or watch.
3. Write your name on the answer sheet.
4. Do not open the question booklet until you are told to do so by the audio instructions.
5. Listen carefully to the audio instructions given.
6. Mark your answers on the answer sheet only.
7. All workings must be completed on a separate piece of paper.
8. You should not use a calculator, dictionary or thesaurus at any point in this paper.
9. Move through the papers as quickly as possible and with care.
10. Follow the instructions at the foot of each page.
11. You should mark your answers with a horizontal strike, as shown on the answer sheet.
12. If you want to change your answer, ensure that you rub out your first answer and that your second answer is clearly more visible.
13. You can go back and review any questions that are within the section you are working on only. You must await further instructions before moving onto another section.

Symbols and Phrases used in the Tests

 Instructions

 Time allowed for this section

 Stop and wait for further instructions

 Continue working

Comprehension

INSTRUCTIONS

 YOU HAVE 8 MINUTES TO COMPLETE THE FOLLOWING SECTION.

YOU HAVE 10 QUESTIONS TO COMPLETE WITHIN THE TIME GIVEN.

EXAMPLES

Comprehension Example

Some people choose to start their Christmas shopping early in October. It has been reported that some people even buy their Christmas presents in the sales in August. In recent years, people have had the option of purchasing their Christmas presents online.

Example 1

According to the passage, what is the earliest that people start their Christmas shopping?

A   In the preceding summer
B   In the preceding October
C   In the preceding November
D   Christmas Eve
E   In early December

The correct answer is A. This has already been marked in Example 1 in the Comprehension section of your answer sheet.

Practice Question 1

What has caused a change in how people shop, in recent years?

A   There are more shops
B   Shops are more crowded
C   You can easily organise your journey to the shops
D   New products are available
E   There has been a rise in use of the Internet

The correct answer is E. Please mark this in Practice Question 1 in the Comprehension section of your answer sheet.

STOP AND WAIT FOR FURTHER INSTRUCTIONS

Summer in St Ives

Edward was a 10-year-old who looked forward to his summer holidays so much. He and his family had been to many places for 'staycations' in recent years, but St Ives for a holiday destination was certainly one of his favourites. He had been there most years, whether it be for just a couple of nights or a week sometimes. He loved so much about the place; the clear blue sea, amazing sandy beaches, delicious seafood, even packing up the car and the long drive down there.

Edward and his three sisters always travelled down by car. Philip drove, and Laura was in the front passenger seat unless Edward was feeling car sick (which happened less often these days), in which case he would be in the front seat. He loved being in the front as he had more space and could control the choice of music. He had made his playlist for the journey, which included all of his current favourite tracks, and a few that everyone would enjoy passing the time on the long journey down to St Ives.

He liked to check the traffic conditions before setting off. His phone informed him that the journey from home was 220 miles and would take about 3 hours 45 minutes. The traffic was usually pretty clear as they left early. If they didn't time it right or there was an incident on the motorway, the journey could take much, much longer – sometimes as long as 7 hours!

Edward enjoyed where the family had chosen to stay in recent years in St Ives, which was an old castle that had been converted into a railway hotel early in the previous century when rail travel to the coast took off. It was situated on top of a hill that overlooked the town of St Ives and the bay. There were sweeping views of the sea from the grounds of the hotel and from the rooms that the family had managed to book several months earlier.

The hotel had such large grounds that it was surrounded by a golf course. Several detached self-catering lodges were dotted around the golf course. These were built from natural materials and blended in well with the environment. They could accommodate 10–12 guests and charged around £3,000 per week in peak season!

Edward enjoyed staying in the hotel, in particular, the lovely buffet breakfasts. They included everything you might fancy for breakfast: eggs, bacon, sausages, beans, a selection of cereals, fruit, yoghurts and delicious pastries. This set you up for the day, and occasionally Edward and his family didn't eat much for the rest of the day until dinner (apart from the odd ice cream in the afternoon on the beach!). Edward had learnt from when he was younger to eat his ice creams fairly quickly, not just because it melted in the glorious sunshine but more a case of avoiding the greedy seagulls that would swoop down and pinch the whole scoop of ice cream in their beaks before you knew it! It only took a couple of incidents like this for Edward to start eating his ice cream in the shop.

The family loved the walk down from the hotel through the dense woodland, alongside a waterfall almost entirely enclosed by some tropical-like plant with enormous leaves. The family enjoyed lovely walks along the coast and secluded bays. The children loved to splash their feet in the sea, make sandcastles and more recently were fascinated with searching the rock pools for little creatures like crabs and small fish. Edward enjoyed visiting the coastguard and lifeguard that were stationed in St Ives; they were certainly kept busy during the bustling peak summer months

CONTINUE WORKING

when St Ives was throbbing with tourists. Occasionally you would hear the distinct sound of the Air Ambulance – a bright yellow helicopter deployed to rescue those in trouble.

The family loved going out for dinner and sampling the lovely fresh fish whilst enjoying the sunset. They had also recently discovered a great burger place down one of the meandering, secluded alleys of old fishermen's cottages just set back from the seafront. The burgers served were enormous and they catered for all different tastes. Edward wasn't sure which he preferred best – the veggie burger or the house special. What he did know was that the walk back up to the hotel after a lazy day at the beach and an enormous burger was never as easy as the walk down!

(1) How many times had Edward been on holiday to St Ives?

A   He has never been to St Ives
B   He has been to St Ives just once
C   This year will be Edward's 12th year in a row of going to St Ives
D   Edward has been to St Ives at least five times already
E   Edward lives in St Ives

(2) How many sisters does Edward have?

A   One
B   Two brothers and one sister
C   Three sisters
D   Four sisters
E   No sisters

(3) How long was the journey from home to St Ives?

A   About 7 miles
B   Usually 7 hours
C   3 hours 15 mins
D   220 miles
E   120 kilometres

(4) Where had the family chosen to stay in St Ives in recent years?

A   The railway station
B   On the train
C   A campsite surrounded by a golf course
D   On the beach
E   In a castle converted into a railway hotel

CONTINUE WORKING ▶

(5) How many guests could stay in one of the detached self-catering cottages around the golf course?

A   Guests were not permitted to stay
B   4 adults and an additional 2 guests on a sofa bed
C   The treehouse could accommodate 8 guests
D   10–12 guests
E   8–10 guests

(6) In the context of the passage, what type of word is 'stationed'? (paragraph 7)

A   Preposition
B   Abstract noun
C   Verb
D   Pronoun
E   Adjective

(7) What obscured the view of the waterfall?

A   Heavy rain
B   Giant cows
C   Large leaves on a tropical plant
D   The mist from the waterfall
E   The finger over the lens

(8) In the context of the passage, what type of word is 'meandering'? (final paragraph)

A   Preposition
B   Adverb
C   Verb
D   Adjective
E   Abstract noun

(9) What did the children enjoy doing on the beach more recently?

A   Searching the rock pools for crabs and small fish
B   Volleyball
C   Digging large holes
D   Burying each other in sand
E   Walking

(10) Using the text, select the option which best answers the following question.

What did Edward find difficult about the holiday?

A   The long drive when the traffic was bad
B   The fact that the sea was so cold
C   The trains that would wake him up early
D   The uphill walk back to the hotel after a day out
E   The bunk beds

STOP AND WAIT FOR FURTHER INSTRUCTIONS

Grammar

INSTRUCTIONS

 YOU HAVE 5 MINUTES TO COMPLETE THE FOLLOWING SECTION.

YOU HAVE 9 QUESTIONS TO COMPLETE WITHIN THE TIME GIVEN.

EXAMPLES

Example 1

The dogs were running in the garden. As the postman opened the gate, the dogs started biting the postman's leg.

Look at the following options taken from the above passage. Select the option that contains a punctuation or grammatical error, if any.

A	B	C	D	E
The dogs	were	in the	garden.	No errors

The correct answer is E. This has already been marked in Example 1 in the Grammar section of your answer sheet.

Practice Question 1

There were several girls in the team. When the team came in after the match, the girls shoes were all piled up outside the door.

Look at the following options taken from the above passage. Select the option that contains a punctuation or grammatical error, if any.

A	B	C	D	E
There were	girls in	the team.	girls shoes	No errors

The correct answer is D. Please mark the answer D in Practice Question 1 in the Grammar section of your answer sheet.

STOP AND WAIT FOR FURTHER INSTRUCTIONS

Look at the following sentences and select the answer from below that has a grammatical or punctuation error, if any.

1 "I'm not sure who's shoes these are."

A	B	C	D	E
"I'm	not sure	who's	shoes	No errors

2 "Me and Sam are going to meet after school."

A	B	C	D	E
"Me and Sam	are going	to meet	after school."	No errors

3 It's use is now in decline as technology has improved.

A	B	C	D	E
It's	use is	technology	has improved.	No errors

4 The two-year guarantee (included free of charge) gave Jack piece of mind with his purchase.

A	B	C	D	E
The two-year	guarantee (included	of charge)	piece of mind	No errors

5 Harry couldn't help thinking that his regular expresso coffees were now becoming a bit of a habit.

A	B	C	D	E
Harry couldn't	his regular	expresso	coffees	No errors

CONTINUE WORKING ▶

6. "If I had known, I would of contacted you earlier."

A	B	C	D	E
"If I	known,	would of	earlier."	No errors

7. "There isn't nobody here," said Jack, worried he had arrived at the wrong time.

A	B	C	D	E
"There	isn't nobody	here,"	Jack, worried	No errors

8. The film effected me greatly, educating me on something I had long been intrigued about.

A	B	C	D	E
effected me	greatly,	me on	long been	No errors

9. There was no doubt that the pupils' work from Class 5C had made a great display for parents' evening.

A	B	C	D	E
no doubt	pupils' work	Class 5C	parents' evening	No errors

STOP AND WAIT FOR FURTHER INSTRUCTIONS ⊗

Numeracy

 INSTRUCTIONS

 YOU HAVE 19 MINUTES TO COMPLETE THE FOLLOWING SECTION.

YOU HAVE 39 QUESTIONS TO COMPLETE WITHIN THE TIME GIVEN.

EXAMPLES

Example 1

Calculate 53 – 42

A   12   **B**   1   **C**   4   **D**   5   **E**   11

The correct answer is E. This has already been marked in Example 1 in the Numeracy section of your answer sheet.

Practice Question 1

Calculate 95 – 75

A   21   **B**   20   **C**   19   **D**   18   **E**   13

The correct answer is B. Please mark this in Practice Question 1 in the Numeracy section of your answer sheet.

STOP AND WAIT FOR FURTHER INSTRUCTIONS ⬡

1 All angles inside a triangle are 60°. The base of the triangle measures 2 cm.

What is the perimeter of the triangle in cm?

A   4   **B**   5   **C**   6   **D**   7   **E**   8

2 What is the order of rotational symmetry of a rectangle?

A   0   **B**   4   **C**   3.5   **D**   1   **E**   2

3 A regular hexagon can be divided into equilateral triangles.

How many equilateral triangles can it be divided into if each of them have a side the same length as a side of the hexagon?

A   6   **B**   5   **C**   4   **D**   7   **E**   8

4 What is the height of a triangle if the base is 4 cm and the area is 32 cm²?

A 10 cm   **B**   16 cm   **C**   12 cm   **D**   11 cm   **E**   15 cm

5 How many m² is a wall measuring 20,000 cm² equivalent to?

A   200   **B**   0   **C**   2   **D**   1   **E**   20

6 Select the appropriate number to take the place of the ? in the sequence below.

123, 112, 102, 93, ?, 78, 72

A   85   **B**   89   **C**   86   **D**   87   **E**   81

7 What is 20% of 120?

A   12   **B**   24   **C**   22   **D**   25   **E**   36

8 Calculate $\frac{2}{3}$ of 36.

A   18   **B**   12   **C**   6   **D**   26   **E**   24

CONTINUE WORKING

9 Tomorrow will be my 16th birthday. Today is April 13th. My brother is currently 3 years younger than me and was born on March 8th. My dad is three times my brother's age now.

How old is my dad now?

A 35 **B** 38 **C** 34 **D** 36 **E** 32

10 What is the size of an exterior angle of a regular octagon?

A 60° **B** 45° **C** 8° **D** 135° **E** 100°

11 How many vertices are there on a tetrahedron?

A 4 **B** 5 **C** 3 **D** 2 **E** 6

12 Calculate the value of a if: $3(a + 1) = 15$

A 10 **B** 12 **C** 15 **D** 4 **E** 5

13 The mean of four numbers is 14. Three of the four numbers are 12, 16 and 14.

What is the value of the fourth number?

A 12 **B** 13 **C** 14 **D** 9 **E** 10

14 Calculate 28 × 17

A 467 **B** 476 **C** 287 **D** 196 **E** 466

15 What is 326.42 divided by 100?

A 32,642 **B** 32.642 **C** 3.2642 **D** 3.3 **E** 3.2462

16 How many 7s can be subtracted from 343?

A 49 **B** 50 **C** 37 **D** 29 **E** 47

CONTINUE WORKING ⇨

17 How fast am I walking if I travel 1.5 miles in half an hour?

   A   2.5 mph   **B**   25 mph   **C**   1.5 mph   **D**   4 mph   **E**   3 mph

18 Which of these numbers has the smallest value?

   A   11.010   **B**   10.110   **C**   10.101   **D**   10.011   **E**   10.0101

19 Which of these numbers has the largest value?

   A   21.011   **B**   21.101   **C**   20.11   **D**   21.01   **E**   21.1

20 A meal deal in a supermarket offers a discount when buying three items together. The deal includes the following three items that are normally priced at:

Fish	£3.99
Mashed potato	£1.75
A vegetable dish	£1.49

The meal deal price is £5.

What is the saving when buying the three items in the meal deal together?

   A   £3.24   **B**   £6.24   **C**   26p   **D**   £2.23   **E**   £2.32

21 Select the appropriate numbers to complete the subtraction in place of the ? in the calculation below.

```
  ? 8 ? 5
- 2 6 7 ?
─────────
  2 ? 0 8
```

The answer options below show the missing numbers as they would appear in the question from left to right.

   A   4, 2, 8, 7   **B**   5, 3, 2, 7   **C**   4, 2, 7, 3

   D   4, 0, 8, 7   **E**   1, 4, 3, 3

CONTINUE WORKING

(22) Select the appropriate numbers to complete the addition in place of the ? in the calculation below.

```
  ? 6 3 ?
+ 1 3 ? 3
─────────
  9 ? 0 1
```

The answer options below show the missing numbers as they would appear in the question from left to right.

A   8, 9, 3, 2   **B**   8, 7, 7, 2   **C**   7, 0, 6, 8
D   7, 9, 1, 8   **E**   8, 9, 7, 8

(23) I walk in a south-west direction to the shops.

When I return home in the opposite direction, what direction am I walking?

A   north-west   **B**   south-east   **C**   north-east
D   south   **E**   south-west

(24) Calculate 372 divided by 6

A   62   **B**   60   **C**   61   **D**   59   **E**   71

(25) What is the total of 372 + 569?

A   951   **B**   841   **C**   931   **D**   941   **E**   851

(26) What is 44% of 80?

A   25.2   **B**   35.2   **C**   32   **D**   36   **E**   32.32

(27) A film finished at 15.50 after lasting for 135 minutes.

At what time did the film start?

A   2.05 p.m.   **B**   2.35 p.m.   **C**   6.05 p.m.
D   1.35 p.m.   **E**   2.15 p.m.

CONTINUE WORKING

(28) A cuboid-shaped box has dimensions as follows:

length 60 cm, width 40 cm, depth 50 cm

What is the volume of the box?

| **A** | 90,000 cm³ | **B** | 12,000 cm³ | **C** | 120,000 cm³ |
| **D** | 72,000 cm³ | **E** | 1.2 m³ | | |

(29) What is the square root of 169?

A   7   **B**   13   **C**   200   **D**   14   **E**   4.3

(30) Each row, column and diagonal of this magic square adds up to the same number.

Complete the magic square by choosing the five numbers to go in the place of a, b, c, d, and e in the correct order.

4	9	d
a	5	e
b	c	6

| **A** | 1, 8, 3, 2, 7 | **B** | 3, 8, 2, 1, 7 | **C** | 3, 8, 1, 2, 7 |
| **D** | 6, 8, 2, 2, 7 | **E** | 3, 2, 7, 2, 7 | | |

(31) A lightbulb box says that the bulb will last for 15,000 hours.

If the bulb is on for an average of 4 hours per day, how long will the bulb last?

| **A** | 3,750 days | **B** | 12 years | **C** | 9 years |
| **D** | 500 weeks | **E** | 1 year | | |

(32) Work out 7,829 − 5,677

A   2,142   **B**   2,132   **C**   2,152   **D**   2,052   **E**   2,252

(33) Ninety-two dogs go for a walk around a park one week. Each dog completes two laps of the park on average.

If one lap of the park is 500 m, how far in total do all of the dogs walk around the park that week?

| **A** | 92 km | **B** | 46 km | **C** | 9,200 m |
| **D** | 4,600 m | **E** | 920,000 m | | |

CONTINUE WORKING

(34) What is a quarter of 0.6?

A   0.1   **B**   0.2   **C**   15   **D**   0.15   **E**   0.125

(35) Calculate 1.25 × 2.2

A   2.25   **B**   2.5   **C**   3   **D**   2.75   **E**   3.25

(36) A special offer box of chocolates has 20% more chocolates than a standard box.

If the special offer box contains 60 chocolates, how many chocolates are in a standard box?

A   72   **B**   45   **C**   55   **D**   48   **E**   50

(37) I spent 20% of my pocket money this month. I saved the rest.

If I saved £40, how much pocket money do I receive each month?

A   £48   **B**   £50   **C**   £10   **D**   £30   **E**   £32

(38) Robert, the robotic vacuum cleaner, is set to clean the house twice daily, at 1 p.m. upstairs and at 1 a.m. downstairs. Robert cleans for 90 minutes before returning to recharge his battery at his charging point.

How long does Robert spend vacuuming in a week?

A   18 hours   **B**   15 hours   **C**   21 hours
D   450 minutes   **E**   540 minutes

(39) Today is the coldest day of the year. The highest temperature during the day is −1° Celsius and the night-time temperature is expected to reach 8 degrees lower.

What is the lowest expected temperature at night?

A   −8° Celsius   **B**   −11° Celsius   **C**   9° Celsius
D   −9° Celsius   **E**   −7° Celsius

STOP AND WAIT FOR FURTHER INSTRUCTIONS ⊗

Synonyms

 INSTRUCTIONS

 YOU HAVE 5 MINUTES TO COMPLETE THE FOLLOWING SECTION.

YOU HAVE 20 QUESTIONS TO COMPLETE WITHIN THE TIME GIVEN.

EXAMPLES

Example 1

Select the word that is most similar in meaning to the following word:

cold

A	B	C	D	E
collect	fence	foggy	windy	chilly

The correct answer is E. This has already been marked in Example 1 in the Synonyms section of your answer sheet.

Practice Question 1

Select the word that is most similar in meaning to the following word:

start

A	B	C	D	E
cramped	begin	free	without	change

The correct answer is B. Please mark this in Practice Question 1 in the Synonyms section of your answer sheet.

STOP AND WAIT FOR FURTHER INSTRUCTIONS

In each question, identify the word in the table that is most similar in meaning to the given word.

(1) symptom

A	B	C	D	E
detain	thimble	tomb	signal	linger

(2) dedicated

A	B	C	D	E
proceed	tabulate	devoted	educated	impulse

(3) relevant

A	B	C	D	E
related	vain	citizen	critic	muggy

(4) concealed

A	B	C	D	E
justice	hidden	ceiling	confrontation	correspond

(5) function

A	B	C	D	E
purpose	prospect	requirement	sea	gumption

(6) opulent

A	B	C	D	E
transparent	ambiguous	branch	trait	sumptuous

CONTINUE WORKING ▶

7 aspirational

A	B	C	D	E
concert	laden	ambitious	perspiration	diagonal

8 diverse

A	B	C	D	E
enlarge	different	climate	fantasy	tenant

9 harmony

A	B	C	D	E
agreement	courage	archive	jeopardy	indication

10 culture

A	B	C	D	E
wonder	brag	lifestyle	notion	friction

11 evaluated

A	B	C	D	E
welfare	literature	reviewed	categorised	complication

12 scent

A	B	C	D	E
elapse	moment	perfume	suit	currency

13 decline

A	B	C	D	E
development	reject	education	factor	omen

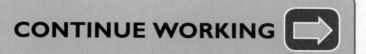

CONTINUE WORKING

14 inclined

A	B	C	D	E
severe	likely	inch	cool	ignite

15 surge

A	B	C	D	E
rush	persuade	jinx	cajole	splurge

16 close

A	B	C	D	E
muggy	distant	flagship	derive	complain

17 explore

A	B	C	D	E
bid	fortunate	dampen	investigate	trend

18 pipped

A	B	C	D	E
beaten	lackadaisical	cipher	partner	trait

19 bumper

A	B	C	D	E
abundant	knowledge	gauge	gaze	season

20 secluded

A	B	C	D	E
scrape	dawn	secret	trickle	doused

STOP AND WAIT FOR FURTHER INSTRUCTIONS

Non-Verbal Reasoning

 YOU HAVE 8 MINUTES TO COMPLETE THE FOLLOWING SECTION.

YOU HAVE 13 QUESTIONS TO COMPLETE WITHIN THE TIME GIVEN.

EXAMPLES

ROTATION Example 1

Select one of the images below that is a rotation of the image on the left.

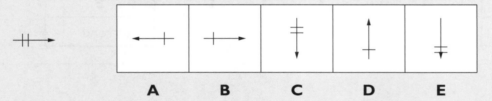

A   **B**   **C**   **D**   **E**

The correct answer is C. This has already been marked in Example 1 in the Non-Verbal Reasoning section of your answer sheet.

ROTATION Practice Question 1

Select one of the images below that is a rotation of the image on the left.

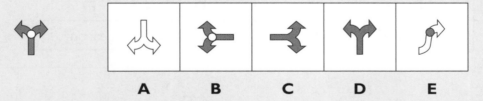

A   **B**   **C**   **D**   **E**

The correct answer is B. Please mark this in Practice Question 1 in the Non-Verbal Reasoning section of your answer sheet.

CONTINUE WORKING ⇨

COMPLETE THE SQUARE Example 2

Which shape or pattern completes the square?

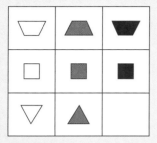 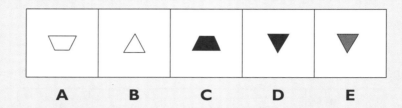

The correct answer is D. This has already been marked in Example 2 in the Non-Verbal Reasoning section of your answer sheet.

COMPLETE THE SQUARE Practice Question 2

Which shape or pattern completes the square?

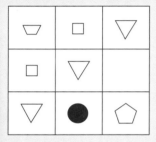 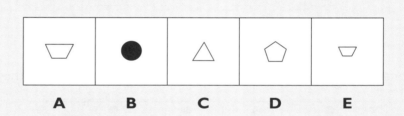

The correct answer is B. Please mark this in Practice Question 2 in the Non-Verbal Reasoning section of your answer sheet.

STOP AND WAIT FOR FURTHER INSTRUCTIONS

1. Select one of the images below that is a rotation of the image on the left.

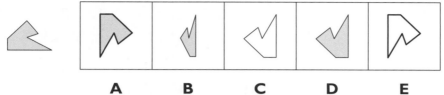

| A | B | C | D | E |

2. Select one of the images below that is a rotation of the image on the left.

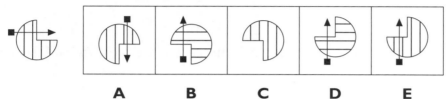

| A | B | C | D | E |

3. Select one of the images below that is a rotation of the image on the left.

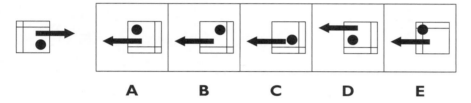

| A | B | C | D | E |

4. Select one of the images below that is a rotation of the image on the left.

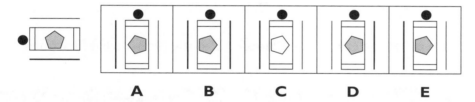

| A | B | C | D | E |

5. Select one of the images below that is a rotation of the image on the left.

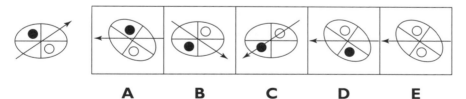

| A | B | C | D | E |

6. Select one of the images below that is a rotation of the image on the left.

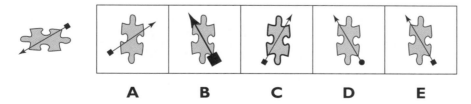

| A | B | C | D | E |

CONTINUE WORKING

7 Which shape or pattern completes the larger square?

A   B   C   D   E

8 Which shape or pattern completes the larger square?

A   B   C   D   E

9 Which shape or pattern completes the larger square?

A   B   C   D   E

10 Which shape or pattern completes the larger square?

A   B   C   D   E

11 Which shape or pattern completes the larger square?

A   B   C   D   E

CONTINUE WORKING

(12) Which shape or pattern completes the larger square?

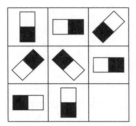
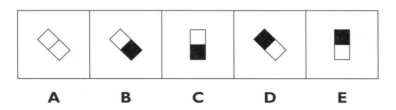

A   B   C   D   E

(13) Which shape or pattern completes the larger square?

A   B   C   D   E

END OF PAPER

Test C Paper 2

Instructions

1. Ensure you have pencils and an eraser with you.

2. Make sure you are able to see a clock or watch.

3. Write your name on the answer sheet.

4. Do not open the question booklet until you are told to do so by the audio instructions.

5. Listen carefully to the audio instructions given.

6. Mark your answers on the answer sheet only.

7. All workings must be completed on a separate piece of paper.

8. You should not use a calculator, dictionary or thesaurus at any point in this paper.

9. Move through the papers as quickly as possible and with care.

10. Follow the instructions at the foot of each page.

11. You should mark your answers with a horizontal strike, as shown on the answer sheet.

12. If you want to change your answer, ensure that you rub out your first answer and that your second answer is clearly more visible.

13. You can go back and review any questions that are within the section you are working on only. You must await further instructions before moving onto another section.

Symbols and Phrases used in the Tests

 Instructions   Time allowed for this section   Stop and wait for further instructions   Continue working

Cloze Sentences

INSTRUCTIONS

 YOU HAVE 7 MINUTES TO COMPLETE THE FOLLOWING SECTION.

YOU HAVE 17 QUESTIONS TO COMPLETE WITHIN THE TIME GIVEN.

EXAMPLES

Example 1

Complete the sentence in the most sensible way by selecting the appropriate word from each set of brackets.

The (dog, big, gate) sat on the (mat, open, great).

A   big, open
B   dog, great
C   gate, mat
D   dog, mat
E   dog, open

The correct answer is D. This has already been marked in Example 1 of the Cloze Sentences section of your answer sheet.

Practice Question 1

Complete the sentence in the most sensible way by selecting the appropriate word from each set of brackets.

My name is (Helen, high, sand) and I am (ten, dig, land) years old.

A   Helen, dig
B   high, land
C   sand, land
D   Helen, land
E   Helen, ten

The correct answer is E. Please mark the answer E in Practice Question 1 in the Cloze Sentences section of your answer sheet.

CONTINUE WORKING

Example 2

One word in the following sentence has had three letters removed from it. Keeping the letters in the same order, identify the three-letter word that is made from these missing letters.

The pupil could not pay attion.

The correct answer is 'ten'. This is shown in Example 2 in the Cloze Sentences section of your answer sheet.

Practice Question 2

One word in the following sentence has had three letters removed from it. Keeping the letters in the same order, identify the three-letter word that is made from these missing letters.

She treasu her mother's bracelet.

The correct answer is 'red'. Please write this in Practice Question 2 in the Cloze Sentences section of your answer sheet.

STOP AND WAIT FOR FURTHER INSTRUCTIONS

Complete the most sensible sentence by selecting the appropriate combination of words from within the brackets. Use one word from each set of brackets.

(1) He was so excited (for, about, to) seeing his (sisters, sister's, mums) new puppy after school.

A	about, sisters
B	for, sisters
C	for, mums
D	to, sisters
E	about, sister's

(2) Based on the (balance, descriptive, evidence), he came to the (brief, assumed, conclusion) that it was indeed the right thing to do.

A	descriptive, conclusion
B	balance, brief
C	evidence, conclusion
D	balance, assumed
E	evidence, brief

CONTINUE WORKING

3 Throughout history, (they're, it's, its) meaning has (evolved, involved, revolved) as language adapted to society.

A   it's, revolved
B   its, evolved
C   they're, involved
D   its, involved
E   it's, involved

4 It is a great (privilege, respectful, honorary) to have been asked to (remove, present, create) this special bravery award to you.

A   honorary, remove
B   honorary, present
C   respectful, present
D   privilege, present
E   privilege, create

5 She was very much looking (for, in, forward) to taking in the sunshine (over, on, bye) a pleasant stroll through the countryside this afternoon.

A   forward, on
B   forward, bye
C   in, on
D   in, over
E   for, on

6 Many (class, pupil, lessons) had been (teach, learned, taught) as a result of her recent experiences.

A   class, taught
B   pupil, learned
C   lessons, learned
D   lessons, taught
E   pupil, teach

7 The (childs, childrens, children's) application of (there, their, they're) knowledge was being tested in this week's quiz.

A   childs, their
B   childs, there
C   childrens, they're
D   childrens, their
E   children's, their

CONTINUE WORKING ▶

(8) He (seldom, partially, highly) went out on his bike as it was almost (under, dark, clearly) when he arrived home from school during the winter months.

A   seldom, dark
B   partially, clearly
C   highly, under
D   seldom, clearly
E   seldom, under

(9) Please (except, inspect, accept) (are, our, hour) apologies for not arriving on time.

A   except, are
B   except, our
C   accept, our
D   accept, are
E   accept, hour

(10) Sam is (especially, special, specific) looking forward (for, in, to) the start of the half-term holidays, as it will be the first time he has been camping.

A   specific, to
B   especially, to
C   special, to
D   special, in
E   especially, in

One word in each of the following sentences has had three letters removed from it. Keeping the letters in the same order, identify the three-letter word that is made from these three missing letters.

(11) The game was postpd until a later date.

(12) Soimes they had dinner a bit later on Fridays.

(13) Jack's parents were tremously proud of what he had achieved.

(14) The boy was described as unkempt and rather scny.

(15) The hosts had been particularly hosable towards their guests.

(16) You would have to have been particularly obsert to have noticed that.

(17) The new neighbour's children became friends instly with other local youngsters.

STOP AND WAIT FOR FURTHER INSTRUCTIONS

Problem Solving

 YOU HAVE 12 MINUTES TO COMPLETE THE FOLLOWING SECTION.

YOU HAVE 10 QUESTIONS TO COMPLETE WITHIN THE TIME GIVEN.

EXAMPLES

A £2.60	B £3.40	C £2.40	D £3.60	E £1.35
F 25	G 14	H 31	I 28	J 34

Example 1

Calculate the following:

If I buy five apples at 20p each, and four bananas at 35p each, how much change will I receive if I pay with a £5 note.

The correct answer is A. This has already been marked in Example 1 in the Problem Solving section of your answer sheet.

Practice Question 1

Calculate the following:

There are 17 people on a bus when it arrives at a bus stop. 11 people get on the bus, and 3 get off. How many people are then left on the bus?

The correct answer is F. Please mark this in Practice Question 1 in the Problem Solving section of your answer sheet.

STOP AND WAIT FOR FURTHER INSTRUCTIONS

A 14	B 15	C 52	D 54	E 1,175
F 10	G 20	H 32	I 50	J 260

Read the passage below, then select an answer to each question from the 10 different possible answers in the table above. You may use an answer for more than one question.

Rosa does her weekly shop at the same supermarket that she works at. She keeps to a strict spending limit as she is trying to save as much money as possible. Every month Rosa is paid £1,000 from her job at the supermarket. As she works there, she receives a 25% discount on everything she spends there. Rosa can afford to spend £60 a week on her shopping after the discount has been deducted.

Rosa works 25 hours each week: from 9 a.m. until 1 p.m. on Monday, Wednesday and Thursday. She also works the night shift stacking shelves from 9 p.m. until 3.30 a.m. on Friday and Saturday nights. Rosa has 5 weeks' holiday each year when she does not work.

Rosa really enjoys her job and has made many friends since starting there on December 1st, last year. Her best friends are twins who work at the supermarket – they are the same age as Rosa but their birthday is exactly 3 weeks before hers.

As well as benefitting from the 25% staff discount, Rosa also looks out for special offers. This week she has seen that the yoghurts she likes are on a special deal of 'buy 3 for the price of 2'. They normally cost 48p each.

Rosa's shop this week has taken a while because she started chatting with the staff that she works with. She came into the supermarket at 9.25 a.m. and left 1 hour and 45 minutes later, although she did have a coffee in the supermarket café while there. Rosa enjoys a coffee every other week at the supermarket at a cost of £2 (after the staff discount).

As she left the store, Rosa checked her receipt and was pleased to see that the 25% discount had reduced her shopping bill by £18. Luckily the shopping was not too heavy because she was cycling home. It is only a distance of 1 mile from the supermarket to her home and the cycle paths are very good. It took her 6 minutes to get home by bicycle from the supermarket.

(1) There are 52 weeks in a year, which is 12 months. Dividing 52 weeks by 12 gives us the number of weeks in an average month, which is $4\frac{1}{3}$ weeks.

After her staff discount, how much can Rosa spend each month in pounds at the supermarket?

(2) If Rosa spends all the money she can afford for shopping in a particular week, how many pounds will she save with her staff discount?

CONTINUE WORKING

(3) What was the cost in pounds of Rosa's shopping this week after the staff discount was deducted (excluding the coffee)?

(4) How much does Rosa spend in pounds on coffees at the supermarket each year?

(5) The twins who are Rosa's friends have their birthday on December 24th.

On which day of January is Rosa's birthday?

(6) The 3-for-2 deal on the yoghurts reduces the cost per yoghurt to how many pence for all shoppers (before any staff discount)?

(7) After allowing for both the offer and the staff discount on the yoghurts, what is the overall percentage discount on the yoghurts for Rosa?

(8) At how many minutes past 11 did Rosa leave the supermarket?

(9) At what speed in miles per hour did Rosa cycle home?

(10) How many hours does Rosa work at the supermarket each year?

STOP AND WAIT FOR FURTHER INSTRUCTIONS ⊗

Antonyms

 YOU HAVE 10 MINUTES TO COMPLETE THE FOLLOWING SECTION.

YOU HAVE 25 QUESTIONS TO COMPLETE WITHIN THE TIME GIVEN.

EXAMPLES

Example 1

Select the word that is least similar to the following word:

light

A	B	C	D	E
dark	water	feather	bright	hill

The correct answer is A. This has already been marked in Example 1 in the Antonyms section of your answer sheet.

Practice Question 1

Select the word that is least similar to the following word:

smooth

A	B	C	D	E
allow	beneath	rough	whilst	shade

The correct answer is C. Please mark the answer C in Practice Question 1 in the Antonyms section of your answer sheet.

STOP AND WAIT FOR FURTHER INSTRUCTIONS

In each row, select the word from the table that is least similar to the word above the table.

1 frightful

A	B	C	D	E
several	spendthrift	mistaken	recuperate	delightful

2 plentiful

A	B	C	D	E
flawed	scarce	tactical	rubric	depressing

3 endangered

A	B	C	D	E
protected	literate	keen	unruly	accuse

4 surrender

A	B	C	D	E
delight	borrow	fight	suspect	grotesque

5 research

A	B	C	D	E
encourage	invent	interrupt	neglect	segregate

6 dexterity

A	B	C	D	E
cleanliness	clumsiness	sadness	indebtedness	suppleness

CONTINUE WORKING

7 gregarious

A	B	C	D	E
frame	tepid	introverted	fluffy	elegant

8 deprive

A	B	C	D	E
indulge	depend	torpid	survive	thrive

9 dutiful

A	B	C	D	E
respectful	eventful	disobedient	envious	phobic

10 abode

A	B	C	D	E
dwelling	disputed	flippant	tenuous	thankful

11 antiquated

A	B	C	D	E
contemporary	spectacular	outgoing	amusing	whole

12 gracious

A	B	C	D	E
beautiful	sedate	wacky	curt	cautious

13 fundamental

A	B	C	D	E
exotic	incidental	aggressive	hurried	fierce

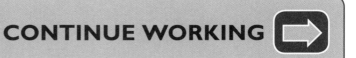

CONTINUE WORKING

(14) archaic

A	B	C	D	E
knowing	jaded	innovative	capable	strange

(15) blossoming

A	B	C	D	E
fading	future	nutty	deceiving	blooming

(16) cajole

A	B	C	D	E
curl	wander	gaze	deter	chop

(17) drastic

A	B	C	D	E
juggle	chivalrous	plentiful	tender	minor

(18) heated

A	B	C	D	E
zany	detailed	seated	rational	breakable

(19) frivolity

A	B	C	D	E
available	prudence	cultured	squeamish	vitality

CONTINUE WORKING ⇨

20 hindrance

A	B	C	D	E
assistance	destruction	arrogance	evidence	harmonious

21 versed

A	B	C	D	E
obtainable	inexperienced	aromatic	thankful	frantic

22 sanctuary

A	B	C	D	E
tendency	conservatory	danger	bogus	empty

23 flabbergasted

A	B	C	D	E
exotic	indifferent	shiny	sincere	abrupt

24 vociferous

A	B	C	D	E
average	spotless	receptive	flexible	mute

25 welcoming

A	B	C	D	E
inspiring	incoming	enchanting	frosty	feigned

STOP AND WAIT FOR FURTHER INSTRUCTIONS

Non-Verbal Reasoning

INSTRUCTIONS

 YOU HAVE 8 MINUTES TO COMPLETE THE FOLLOWING SECTION.

YOU HAVE 15 QUESTIONS TO COMPLETE WITHIN THE TIME GIVEN.

EXAMPLES

COMPLETE THE SQUARE Example 1

Which shape or pattern completes the larger square?

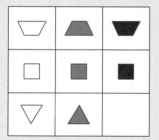
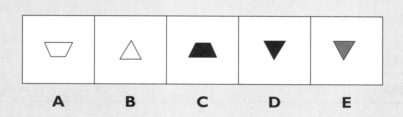

The correct answer is D. This has already been marked in Example 1 in the Non-Verbal Reasoning section of your answer sheet.

COMPLETE THE SQUARE Practice Question 1

Which shape or pattern completes the larger square?

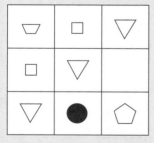
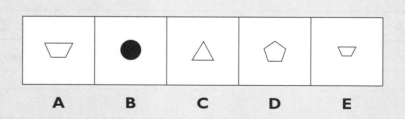

The correct answer is B. Please mark this in Practice Question 1 in the Non-Verbal Reasoning section of your answer sheet.

CONTINUE WORKING ➡

REFLECTION Example 2

Select an image from the row below that shows how the shape or pattern on the left will appear when reflected.

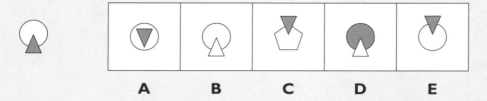

The correct answer is E. This has already been marked in Example 2 in the Non-Verbal Reasoning section of your answer sheet.

REFLECTION Practice Question 2

Select an image from the row below that shows how the shape or pattern on the left will appear when reflected.

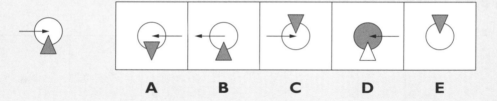

The correct answer is C. Please mark this in Practice Question 2 in the Non-Verbal Reasoning section of your answer sheet.

STOP AND WAIT FOR FURTHER INSTRUCTIONS

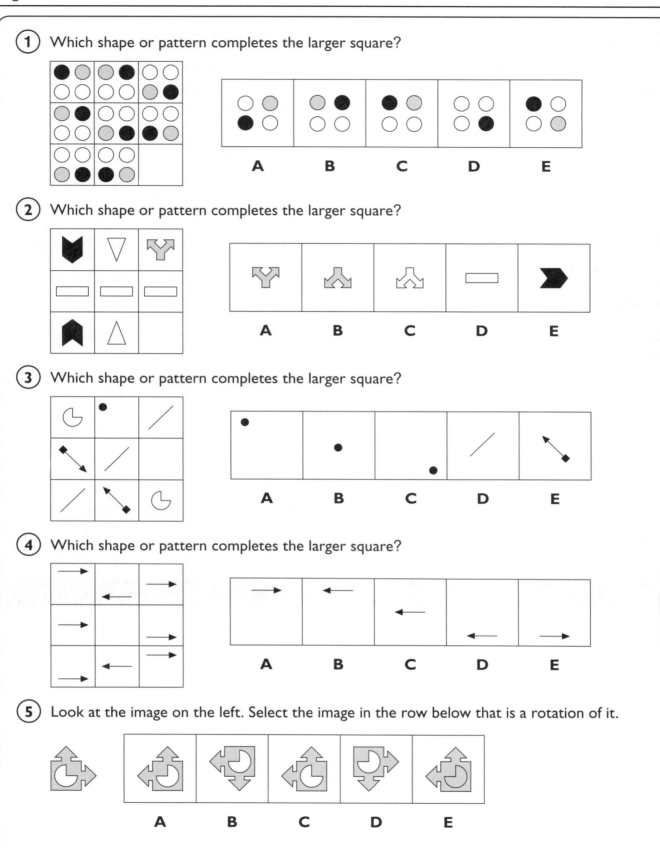

1 Which shape or pattern completes the larger square?

A   B   C   D   E

2 Which shape or pattern completes the larger square?

A   B   C   D   E

3 Which shape or pattern completes the larger square?

A   B   C   D   E

4 Which shape or pattern completes the larger square?

A   B   C   D   E

5 Look at the image on the left. Select the image in the row below that is a rotation of it.

A   B   C   D   E

CONTINUE WORKING

6 Look at the image on the left. Select the image in the row below that is a rotation of it.

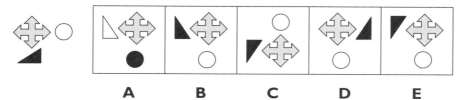

7 Look at the image on the left. Select the image in the row below that is a rotation of it.

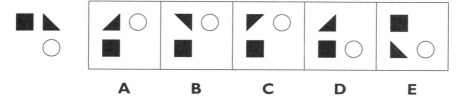

8 Look at the image on the left. Select the image in the row below that is a rotation of it.

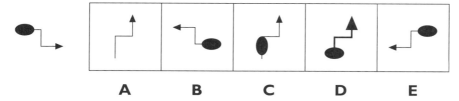

9 Select an image from the row below that shows how the shape or pattern on the left will appear when reflected.

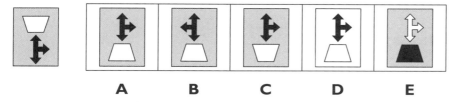

10 Select an image from the row below that shows how the shape or pattern on the left will appear when reflected.

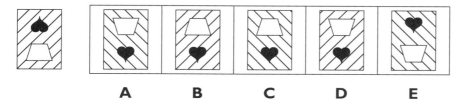

CONTINUE WORKING ➡

⑪ Select an image from the row below that shows how the shape or pattern on the left will appear when reflected.

| | A | B | C | D | E |

⑫ Select an image from the row below that shows how the shape or pattern on the left will appear when reflected.

| | A | B | C | D | E |

⑬ Select an image from the row below that shows how the shape or pattern on the left will appear when reflected.

| | A | B | C | D | E |

⑭ Select the picture from below that will complete the sequence in place of the ?

| | A | B | C | D | E |

⑮ Select the picture from below that will complete the sequence in place of the ?

| | A | B | C | D | E |

STOP AND WAIT FOR FURTHER INSTRUCTIONS

Shuffled Sentences

INSTRUCTIONS

 YOU HAVE 8 MINUTES TO COMPLETE THE FOLLOWING SECTION.

YOU HAVE 15 QUESTIONS TO COMPLETE WITHIN THE TIME GIVEN.

EXAMPLES

Example 1

The following sentence is shuffled and also contains one unnecessary word. Rearrange the sentence correctly, in order to identify the unnecessary word.

dog the ran fetch the to stick gluing.

A	B	C	D	E
gluing	dog	ran	the	stick

The correct answer is A. This has already been marked in Example 1 in the Shuffled Sentences section of your answer sheet.

Practice Question 1

The following sentence is shuffled and also contains one unnecessary word. Rearrange the sentence correctly, in order to identify the unnecessary word.

pushed Emma stood up and closed the table under the chairs.

A	B	C	D	E
chairs	stood	under	closed	Emma

The correct answer is D. Please mark this in Practice Question 1 in the Shuffled Sentences section of your answer sheet.

STOP AND WAIT FOR FURTHER INSTRUCTIONS

The following sentence is shuffled and also contains one unnecessary word. Rearrange the sentence correctly, in order to identify the unnecessary word.

(1) to the poor farmer he was rich gave because the money given

A	B	C	D	E
rich	given	poor	money	gave

(2) to bake is bread role a roll of the baker

A	B	C	D	E
roll	role	bread	bake	baker

(3) from the garden water plants petal she rose her comfortable to seat

A	B	C	D	E
rose	plants	seat	petal	from

(4) all of name must wear labels be uniform sewn onto items

A	B	C	D	E
uniform	must	wear	items	of

(5) she had past six test attempting to pass spent her driving the months passed

A	B	C	D	E
pass	passed	past	spent	test

(6) to tear the present she had unwrapped eye that brought her a paper

A	B	C	D	E
eye	unwrapped	brought	paper	tear

(7) of tune the wind blow was out of the orchestra section

A	B	C	D	E
section	tune	orchestra	wind	blow

CONTINUE WORKING

(8) her key hole get in she couldn't had lost she because

A	B	C	D	E
lost	hole	key	get	in

(9) the night in the telescope diamonds shone sky like stars

A	B	C	D	E
diamonds	stars	telescope	shone	sky

(10) to drive a road is illegal licence it a car without

A	B	C	D	E
road	Illegal	licence	without	drive

(11) to suitcase everything he tried the juice squeeze into

A	B	C	D	E
into	tried	squeeze	suitcase	juice

(12) in the afternoon I stuck jam strawberry a traffic spent

A	B	C	D	E
in	strawberry	stuck	spent	afternoon

(13) no longer could she rudeness tolerated be her

A	B	C	D	E
longer	be	her	she	rudeness

(14) he was released train so busy caught the next his usual one

A	B	C	D	E
he	busy	caught	released	next

(15) in the knife until they fork followed the signs they came to a road

A	B	C	D	E
fork	signs	knife	signs	followed

END OF PAPER

Test D Paper 1

Instructions

1. Ensure you have pencils and an eraser with you.

2. Make sure you are able to see a clock or watch.

3. Write your name on the answer sheet.

4. Do not open the question booklet until you are told to do so by the audio instructions.

5. Listen carefully to the audio instructions given.

6. Mark your answers on the answer sheet only.

7. All workings must be completed on a separate piece of paper.

8. You should not use a calculator, dictionary or thesaurus at any point in this paper.

9. Move through the papers as quickly as possible and with care.

10. Follow the instructions at the foot of each page.

11. You should mark your answers with a horizontal strike, as shown on the answer sheet.

12. If you want to change your answer, ensure that you rub out your first answer and that your second answer is clearly more visible.

13. You can go back and review any questions that are within the section you are working on only. You must await further instructions before moving onto another section.

Symbols and Phrases used in the Tests

 Instructions

 Time allowed for this section

 Stop and wait for further instructions

 Continue working

Comprehension

 INSTRUCTIONS

 YOU HAVE 10 MINUTES TO COMPLETE THE FOLLOWING SECTION.

YOU HAVE 14 QUESTIONS TO COMPLETE WITHIN THE TIME GIVEN.

EXAMPLES

Comprehension Example

Some people choose to start their Christmas shopping early in October. It has been reported that some people even buy their Christmas presents in the sales in August. In recent years, people have had the option of purchasing their Christmas presents online.

Example 1

According to the passage, what is the earliest that people start their Christmas shopping?

A   In the preceding summer
B   In the preceding October
C   In the preceding November
D   Christmas Eve
E   In early December

The correct answer is A. This has already been marked in Example 1 in the Comprehension section of your answer sheet.

Practice Question 1

In recent years, what has caused a change in how people shop?

A   There are more shops
B   Shops are more crowded
C   You can easily organise your journey to the shops
D   New products are available
E   There has been a rise in use of the Internet

The correct answer is E. Please mark this in Practice Question 1 in the Comprehension section of your answer sheet.

STOP AND WAIT FOR FURTHER INSTRUCTIONS

Read the following passage, then answer the questions below.

An Unlikely Confession

"You can't do that, you'll get into trouble," warned Norman.

Ellie ignored the well-meant warnings of her younger brother, and continued in her attempts to prize open the antique looking trunk that they had found in the restricted area of the garage. Although the children were allowed in the garage, entrance to this particular area was strictly prohibited because of the sharp garden tools which hung from the protruding nails above their heads. Today their parents had gone out and left them alone for the first time; a trial, they called it. Norman was determined to be sensible, and prove that they could be trusted 'home alone'. His school friends were often left alone and he saw this as the first step towards being an adult. Ellie on the other hand, despite being the elder sibling, had no ambitions to be an adult and believed that, when the cat's away, the mice will play.

"I can't get it open," sighed Ellie with a decidedly frustrated expression on her face. The trunk was refusing to reveal its contents; it looked as though it hadn't been opened for years. The rusty mechanism had jammed and no amount of poking seemed to be working. In fact, the more Ellie prodded it with the bent wire she had fashioned into a key, the more stuck it looked. It was unlikely it would ever open again.

"Leave it alone, you're going to break it and you're not even supposed to be here," whispered a fraught looking Norman between sideways glances.

"If you help me work out how to get it open, I'll be finished a lot quicker. After all, two heads are better than one," remarked Ellie.

"Why have you got such a bee in your bonnet about that box anyway?" asked Norman.

"I don't know, maybe it's because I'm not allowed to see inside, it makes me all the more curious. Aren't you curious too?" asked Ellie.

"No! I'm not, and one day this sort of irresponsible behaviour is going to land you in hot water, you'll see," replied Norman. His voice was starting to rise as he became increasingly annoyed with his older sister.

"Oh, stop being such a wet blanket will you. No one's going to find out," snapped Ellie.

Just at that moment, the children heard the sound of a car pulling into the driveway. They stood frozen to the spot as car doors slammed shut, and then the familiar sound of a woman's heels were heard entering the house adjacent to the garage. Ellie's care-free demeanour changed suddenly as the reality of the situation hit home.

"Help me put it back, Norman. Come on, we're in the same boat. Do you want to get into trouble?" said Ellie.

"It's your problem, not mine. As you made your bed, you must now lie in it," replied a rather smug Norman. As soon as he had spoken, he regretted it. His sister had really been through the mill recently and he had promised his parents he would be supportive. Surely they hadn't meant he should support her in a situation like this though.

CONTINUE WORKING ▶

"Look," Ellie was pleading now, "if you help me now I promise I'll turn over a new leaf – just help me put this back."

The sound of footsteps in the hallway had stopped and the silence was even more worrying. Knowing that just by being there he was complicit in the deception, Norman hastily helped Ellie to slide the trunk back into its resting place. As the door handle to the garage started to move, Ellie and Norman escaped into the back garden through the side door. A few minutes later they strolled through the back door of the house as if nothing had happened.

"There you are," said their mother. "I was beginning to think you were up to no good. Well everything seems to be in order, the trial has obviously gone well. Well done, I'm proud of you. You're both so grown-up now."

Ellie smiled, relieved that she had once again got away with it, but she could see that her brother wasn't smiling. Was he going to let the cat out of the bag? Norman's mouth started to open and Ellie's grin turned to a look of horror. Before he could utter a sound, the door opened and in walked their father who had returned from the Post Office collection depot with a large cardboard box. He announced that it was for Ellie. What a mystery! She wasn't expecting anything. As she knelt on the floor to open the box surrounded by her family, she felt an unfamiliar feeling. This box opened willingly revealing a beautiful new dress and the card read, "something to cheer you up, love from Mum, Dad and Norm". She loved the dress yet tears were starting to well up in her eyes. She had become accustomed to her family's attentiveness since the diagnosis, however this was different. She knew she had to make a clean breast of it.

(1) Which phrase best describes the restricted zone in the garage?

    A   An area where dangerous garden equipment is stored safely out of the children's reach
    B   A space reserved for car equipment and parking only
    C   Their father's workshop
    D   A family games room
    E   A space for chemical storage, a safe distance from the living area

(2) Which word best describes Norman's feelings?

    A   Curious
    B   Anxious
    C   Vivacious
    D   Disappointed
    E   Nonchalant

CONTINUE WORKING ⬛➡

3 In the context of the text, what is the meaning of the proverb, 'When the cat's away, the mice will play'?

A They have a vermin problem in the garage
B Mice are a problem when the cat leaves the house
C They need to bring in a pest control specialist
D Without adult supervision the children will do what they like
E When the family is away, the animals take over the house

4 Why was Ellie so eager to open the box?

A She was frantically looking for something she had lost
B She was looking for an old bonnet
C She was looking for a favourite blanket
D It contained her baby blankets
E She was intrigued by the mystery

5 What is meant by the phrase 'to have a bee in one's bonnet'?

A To act haughtily
B To feel uncomfortable in one's clothing
C To be followed by a persistent insect
D To demonstrate obsessive behaviour
E To misbehave

6 What did Ellie mean when she called her brother a 'wet blanket'?

A His negativity was spoiling her fun
B He looked cold and was making her feel uncomfortable
C He had spilt water on the box that Ellie was trying to open
D She thought his clothes were ugly and unfashionable
E She thought he was being arrogant

7 How did Ellie try to persuade Norman to help her?

A She offered to give him her favourite toy boat
B She offered him her pocket money
C She paid him in sweets
D She pestered him continuously until he acceded
E She reminded him that, if found out, he would be in as much trouble as her

CONTINUE WORKING

8 What type of word is 'mystery' (final paragraph)?

- **A** Abstract noun
- **B** Adjective
- **C** Adverb
- **D** Preposition
- **E** Conjunction

9 What is the meaning of the proverb 'as you make your bed, you must now lie in it'?

- **A** You are unkind
- **B** You should make your bed in the mornings
- **C** You are untidy
- **D** You have to accept the consequences of your actions
- **E** You look tired, you should get more sleep

10 Why did Ellie's manner change when her mother returned home?

- **A** She was angry that Norman was unwilling to help
- **B** She was annoyed that she hadn't managed to open the trunk in time
- **C** She realised how much trouble she would be in if discovered
- **D** She was worried that she might accidentally get locked in the garage as no one knew they were there
- **E** She realised that she hadn't completed her chores in time

11 Why did Norman regret his harsh words when Ellie had asked for help?

- **A** Ellie had been ill recently and Norman was supposed to be supporting her through a difficult time
- **B** Ellie had started to cry when Norman shouted at her
- **C** Norman was worried that Ellie would tell their parents he had been unkind to her and he would be in trouble
- **D** Ellie had a tendency to become uncontrollably angry when Norman shouted at her
- **E** He was worried his parents might overhear and reprimand him for being unkind

12 In the context of the text, what is the meaning of the word 'complicit'?

- **A** Exempt from any blame
- **B** Involved in some wrongdoing along with others
- **C** Responsible
- **D** Irreproachable
- **E** Helpless

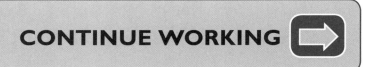

CONTINUE WORKING

13 Which word best describes Ellie's unfamiliar feeling (final paragraph)?

A   Envy

B   Triumph

C   Guilt

D   Vexation

E   Resentment

14 What does the text suggest that Ellie might have done next?

A   Confessed to having been in the prohibited area of the garage and trying to open the trunk

B   Asked her parents for the key to the mystery trunk in the garage

C   Lied about being in the garage

D   Told her parents that Norman had been in the restricted area of the garage trying to open a locked trunk

E   Tried on her new dress

STOP AND WAIT FOR FURTHER INSTRUCTIONS ⊗

Numeracy

INSTRUCTIONS

 YOU HAVE 17 MINUTES TO COMPLETE THE FOLLOWING SECTION.

YOU HAVE 28 QUESTIONS TO COMPLETE WITHIN THE TIME GIVEN.

EXAMPLES

Example 1

Calculate 53 – 42

A 12 **B** 1 **C** 4 **D** 5 **E** 11

The correct answer is E. This has already been marked in Example 1 in the Numeracy section of your answer sheet.

Practice Question 1

Calculate 95 – 75

A 21 **B** 20 **C** 19 **D** 18 **E** 13

The correct answer is B. Please mark this in Practice Question 1 in the Numeracy section of your answer sheet.

STOP AND WAIT FOR FURTHER INSTRUCTIONS

(**1**) If $a = 5$, calculate $2a + 1$

A 11 **B** 25 **C** 26 **D** 53 **E** 9

(**2**) Work out $5^2 - 4^2$

A 9 **B** 25 **C** 16 **D** 41 **E** 11

③ $\frac{1}{8}$ of 176 is:

A   102   **B**   22   **C**   170   **D**   1,408   **E**   168

④ What is the size of each interior angle in a hexagon?

A	72 degrees	**B**	120 degrees	**C**	105 degrees
D	60 degrees	**E**	150 degrees		

⑤ Find a, if $b = 2a - 4$, and $b = 16$

A   0   **B**   6   **C**   14   **D**   2   **E**   10

⑥ If $b = 6$, find a using the following equation:

$12a - b = 0$

A   0.5   **B**   2   **C**   0   **D**   6   **E**   7

⑦ Find the missing number marked by the ?

$8 \times 2 + ? = 32$

A   2   **B**   4   **C**   16   **D**   17   **E**   10

⑧ Find the missing number marked by the ?

$4 + 8 \div ? = 6$

A   2   **B**   4   **C**   6   **D**   8   **E**   10

⑨ Find the missing number marked by the ?

$? + 5 \times 2 = 40$

A   6   **B**   5   **C**   20   **D**   4   **E**   30

⑩ Wrapping paper costs £2.50 per metre. Each roll is 3 m long.

How many rolls can I buy for £15?

A   6   **B**   3   **C**   2   **D**   15   **E**   30

CONTINUE WORKING ⇨

11 I have just tossed a coin. The coin shows a head.

What is the probability that the next time I toss the coin, I will get a head?

A   1 in 2   **B**   1 in 3   **C**   1 in 4

D   impossible   **E**   certain

12 Calculate the answer to the following:

$(28 \div 4) + 8 - 11 = ?$

A   7   **B**   4   **C**   15   **D**   26   **E**   3

13 What is $\frac{3}{7}$ of 49?

A   21   **B**   14   **C**   7   **D**   349   **E**   0

14 What is the number in this sequence marked by a '?'

12, 8, 14, 7, 16, 6, ?

A   6   **B**   7   **C**   18   **D**   20   **E**   5

15 Edward is 2 years younger than Holly.

Rosa is $\frac{1}{5}$ of Edward's current age.

Isla is 5 years older than Rosa.

If Isla is 7, how old is Holly?

A   12   **B**   10   **C**   8   **D**   2   **E**   7

16 I have 42 sweets that I am sharing out between me and my 6 friends.

How many sweets do we each receive?

A   7   **B**   8   **C**   6   **D**   5   **E**   10

17 The buses always arrive on time at the bus stop. There are two different bus routes that I could catch to school.

Bus A arrives every 8 minutes. Bus B arrives every 12 minutes. The first buses both arrive at the bus stop at 7.30 a.m. I arrive at 8 a.m.

How many minutes will I have to wait until both buses arrive at the same time at the bus stop?

A   24   **B**   18   **C**   16   **D**   32   **E**   5

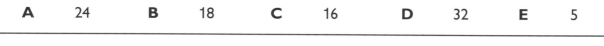

CONTINUE WORKING

(18) Work out the number in this sequence marked by a '?'

3, 17, 5, 20, 7, 23, 9, ?

A   11   **B**   10   **C**   25   **D**   26   **E**   27

(19) Which of the following is smallest in value?

one quarter of 248   one fifth of 70   one tenth of 142   half of 27   one third of 40

A   one quarter of 248   **B**   one fifth of 70   **C**   one tenth of 142
D   half of 27   **E**   one third of 40

(20) There are 15 people on a train. After a while, 3 of these people get off the train, and a further 7 people board the train.

How many people are now on the train?

A   25   **B**   11   **C**   19   **D**   22   **E**   12

Questions 21–23 questions relate to the chart shown below:

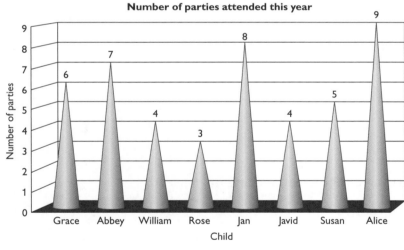

Number of parties attended this year

(21) What is the range of this information?

A   7   **B**   9   **C**   4   **D**   1   **E**   6

(22) What is the mean number of parties attended?

A   5.75   **B**   4.75   **C**   5.5   **D**   5   **E**   4.26

CONTINUE WORKING

23 What is the median number of parties attended?

A   4.5   **B**   3   **C**   5.5   **D**   4   **E**   9

Questions 24–28 relate to the chart shown below:

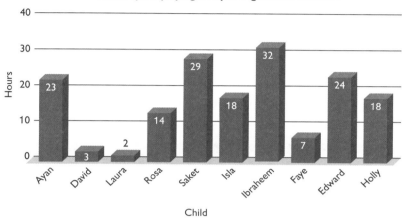

Hours spent playing computer games in a month

24 What is the median number of hours spent playing computer games?

A   18   **B**   20.5   **C**   23.5   **D**   20   **E**   17

25 What is the mode number of hours spent playing computer games?

A   17   **B**   22   **C**   18   **D**   32   **E**   2

26 What is the mean number of hours spent playing computer games?

A   17   **B**   18   **C**   16   **D**   19   **E**   20

27 Calculate the range of the information.

A   31   **B**   30   **C**   32   **D**   23   **E**   26

28 Which of the following people spent the most time playing computer games?

A   Holly and Edward
B   Rosa and Ibraheem
C   Laura, Isla and Rosa
D   Ibraheem and Saket
E   Saket, Laura and Holly

STOP AND WAIT FOR FURTHER INSTRUCTIONS

Synonyms

INSTRUCTIONS

 YOU HAVE 9 MINUTES TO COMPLETE THE FOLLOWING SECTION.

YOU HAVE 20 QUESTIONS TO COMPLETE WITHIN THE TIME GIVEN.

EXAMPLES

Example 1

Select the word that is most similar in meaning to the following word:

cold

A	B	C	D	E
collect	fence	foggy	windy	chilly

The correct answer is E. This has already been marked in Example 1 in the Synonyms section of your answer sheet.

Practice Question 1

Select the word that is most similar in meaning to the following word:

start

A	B	C	D	E
cramped	begin	free	without	change

The correct answer is B. Please mark this in Practice Question 1 in the Synonyms section of your answer sheet.

STOP AND WAIT FOR FURTHER INSTRUCTIONS

In each row, identify the word in the table that is most similar in meaning to the word above the table.

① coy

A	B	C	D	E
crazed	classic	shy	company	notion

② despise

A	B	C	D	E
hone	revise	hasten	hate	respite

③ intermittent

A	B	C	D	E
morose	fragile	periodic	continual	believable

④ pompous

A	B	C	D	E
stationary	subdued	leader	helix	conceited

⑤ recall

A	B	C	D	E
tranquil	remember	persevere	quarrel	seldom

⑥ altitude

A	B	C	D	E
height	attitude	confrontation	tardy	lethargic

CONTINUE WORKING ⇨

7 summit

A	B	C	D	E
mishap	peak	spasm	vulgar	sphere

8 intrepid

A	B	C	D	E
scent	foul	precious	adventurous	admiration

9 banal

A	B	C	D	E
boring	overlook	residents	fragment	canal

10 mutual

A	B	C	D	E
beautiful	whine	empty	shared	abnormal

11 incredulous

A	B	C	D	E
triumph	impoverished	unbelievable	deplorable	squalid

12 polarised

A	B	C	D	E
threat	galaxy	beyond	divided	avid

13 debrief

A	B	C	D	E
entrepreneur	review	sustain	reveal	tantalise

CONTINUE WORKING

14 portrayed

A	B	C	D	E
picturesque	detained	sequential	reluctant	depicted

15 gesture

A	B	C	D	E
gentrified	measly	act	delectable	habitat

16 token

A	B	C	D	E
symbol	emotive	series	demolish	haphazard

17 baffled

A	B	C	D	E
attentive	afraid	delicate	urgency	bewildered

18 preceding

A	B	C	D	E
revealing	generous	following	earlier	heightened

19 affectionate

A	B	C	D	E
nippy	loving	damp	barren	legalise

20 glut

A	B	C	D	E
excess	summary	destiny	stable	effect

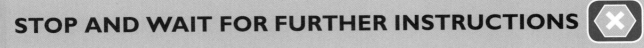

STOP AND WAIT FOR FURTHER INSTRUCTIONS

Non-Verbal Reasoning

 YOU HAVE 9 MINUTES TO COMPLETE THE FOLLOWING SECTION.

YOU HAVE 15 QUESTIONS TO COMPLETE WITHIN THE TIME GIVEN.

EXAMPLES

REFLECTION Example 1

Select an image from the row below that shows how the shape or pattern on the left will appear when reflected.

A   B   C   D   E

The correct answer is E. This has already been marked in Example 1 in the Non-Verbal Reasoning section of your answer sheet.

REFLECTION Practice Question 1

Select an image from the row below that shows how the shape or pattern on the left will appear when reflected.

A   B   C   D   E

The correct answer is C. Please mark this in Practice Question 1 in the Non-Verbal Reasoning section of your answer sheet.

CONTINUE WORKING ➡

ROTATION Example 2

Select an image from the row below that is a rotation of the image on the left.

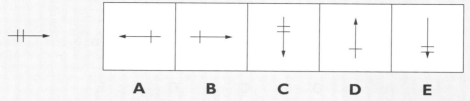

The correct answer is C. This has already been marked in Example 2 in the Non-Verbal Reasoning section of your answer sheet.

ROTATION Practice Question 2

Select an image from the row below that is a rotation of the image on the left.

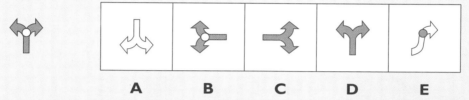

The correct answer is B. Please mark this in Practice Question 2 in the Non-Verbal Reasoning section of your answer sheet.

LEAST SIMILAR Example 3

Select the image that is least similar to the other images.

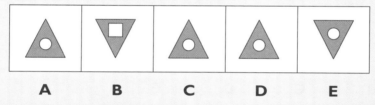

The correct answer is B. This has already been marked in Example 3 in the Non-Verbal Reasoning section of your answer sheet.

LEAST SIMILAR Practice Question 3

Select the image that is least similar to the other images.

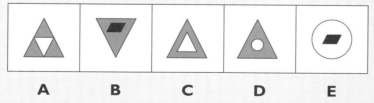

The correct answer is E. Please mark this in Practice Question 3 in the Non-Verbal Reasoning section of your answer sheet.

STOP AND WAIT FOR FURTHER INSTRUCTIONS ⊗

1. Select one of the images below that is a rotation of the image on the left.

A   B   C   D   E

2. Select one of the images below that is a rotation of the image on the left.

A   B   C   D   E

3. Select the image that is least similar to the others in the row.

A   B   C   D   E

4. Select the image that is least similar to the others in the row.

A   B   C   D   E

5. Select the image that is least similar to the others in the row.

A   B   C   D   E

6. Select the image that is least similar to the others in the row.

A   B   C   D   E

CONTINUE WORKING ⏩

(7) Select the image that is least similar to the others in the row.

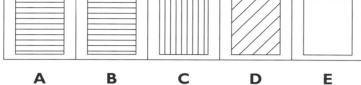

A   B   C   D   E

(8) Select the image that is least similar to the others in the row.

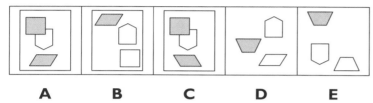

A   B   C   D   E

(9) Select the image that is least similar to the others in the row.

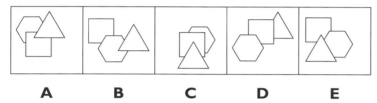

A   B   C   D   E

(10) Select the image that is least similar to the others in the row.

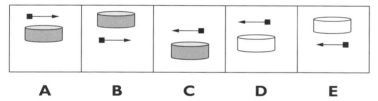

A   B   C   D   E

(11) Select the image that is least similar to the others in the row.

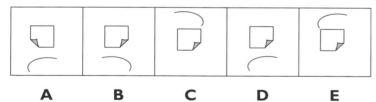

A   B   C   D   E

(12) Select the image that is least similar to the others in the row.

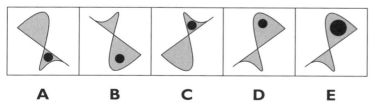

A   B   C   D   E

CONTINUE WORKING ⇨

(13) Select an image from the row below that shows how the shape or pattern on the left could appear when reflected:

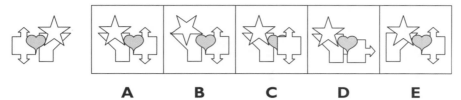

| A | B | C | D | E |

(14) Select an image from the row below that shows how the shape or pattern on the left could appear when reflected:

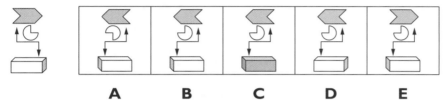

| A | B | C | D | E |

(15) Select an image from the row below that shows how the shape or pattern on the left could appear when reflected:

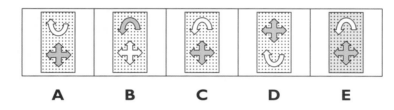

| A | B | C | D | E |

END OF PAPER

Test D Paper 2

Instructions

1. Ensure you have pencils and an eraser with you.

2. Make sure you are able to see a clock or watch.

3. Write your name on the answer sheet.

4. Do not open the question booklet until you are told to do so by the audio instructions.

5. Listen carefully to the audio instructions given.

6. Mark your answers on the answer sheet only.

7. All workings must be completed on a separate piece of paper.

8. You should not use a calculator, dictionary or thesaurus at any point in this paper.

9. Move through the papers as quickly as possible and with care.

10. Follow the instructions at the foot of each page.

11. You should mark your answers with a horizontal strike, as shown on the answer sheet.

12. If you want to change your answer, ensure that you rub out your first answer and that your second answer is clearly more visible.

13. You can go back and review any questions that are within the section you are working on only. You must await further instructions before moving onto another section.

Symbols and Phrases used in the Tests

 Instructions  Time allowed for this section   Stop and wait for further instructions   Continue working

Cloze Sentences

 INSTRUCTIONS

 YOU HAVE 7 MINUTES TO COMPLETE THE FOLLOWING SECTION.

YOU HAVE 17 QUESTIONS TO COMPLETE WITHIN THE TIME GIVEN.

EXAMPLES

A	B	C	D	E	F	G	H	I	J
dog	small	tiny	huge	minute	free	big	enormous	gigantic	penguin

Example 1

Complete the sentence in the most sensible way by selecting an appropriate word from the table above.

The _____ sat by the fire.

The correct answer is A. This has already been marked in Example 1 in the Cloze Sentences section of your answer sheet.

Practice Question 1

Complete the sentence in the most sensible way by selecting an appropriate word from the table above.

The _____ laid an egg.

The correct answer is J. Please mark the answer J in Practice Question 1 in the Cloze Sentences section of your answer sheet.

Example 2

One word in the following sentence has had three letters removed from it. Keeping the letters in the same order, identify the three-letter word that is made from the missing letters.

The pupil could not pay attion.

The correct answer is 'ten'. This has been marked in Example 2 in the Cloze Sentences section of your answer sheet.

CONTINUE WORKING

Practice Question 2

One word in the following sentence has had three letters removed from it. Keeping the letters in the same order, identify the three-letter word that is made from the missing letters.

She treasu her mother's bracelet.

The correct answer is 'red'. Please mark this in Practice Question 2 in the Cloze Sentences section of your answer sheet.

STOP AND WAIT FOR FURTHER INSTRUCTIONS

Complete the most sensible sentence by selecting an appropriate word from the table below.

A laceration	B obdurate	C intricate	D irritable	E defunct
F affability	G disdain	H emphatic	I toil	J nostalgia

(1) He was _____ in his assertion of what he saw.

(2) His _____ was so endearing to people allowing him to forge many friendships.

(3) He was so _____ that he refused to sign the agreement.

(4) The now _____ operating system on the phone required an update.

(5) Her grandmother has _____ for the past.

(6) He looked at his mother with _____ as she suggested wearing his older brother's school uniform rather than buying a completely new uniform.

(7) The lack of sleep over recent days had caused him to become rather _____ .

CONTINUE WORKING

(8) As a result of falling from her bike, she had a _____ on her knee.

(9) He admired the _____ detail used to finish the piece.

(10) The many months of _____ had certainly paid off and he was proud of his achievement.

One word in the following sentence has had three letters removed from it. Keeping the letters in the same order, identify the three-letter word that is made from these three missing letters.

(11) The shoppers jost as they eagerly searched for bargains in the bustling shop.

(12) Sarah was happy ling her pen to Jack as long as he returned it.

(13) The regention of the town centre by the local authority was long overdue.

(14) Her school teachers had always known Ella was desed for great things.

(15) Andy thought the new boy to join the class was rather pretious.

(16) The new bch of the business had been established during the recent turbulent times.

(17) For a fleeg moment I saw a rabbit up ahead among the trees.

STOP AND WAIT FOR FURTHER INSTRUCTIONS ✖

Problem Solving

 YOU HAVE 12 MINUTES TO COMPLETE THE FOLLOWING SECTION.

YOU HAVE 10 QUESTIONS TO COMPLETE WITHIN THE TIME GIVEN.

EXAMPLES

A £2.60	B £3.40	C £2.40	D £3.60	E £1.35
F 25	G 14	H 31	I 28	J 34

Example 1

Calculate the following:

If I buy five apples at 20p each, and four bananas at 35p each, how much change will I receive if I pay with a £5 note.

The correct answer is A. This has already been marked in Example 1 in the Problem Solving section of your answer sheet.

Practice Question 1

Calculate the following:

There are 17 people on a bus when it arrives at a bus stop. 11 people get on the bus, and 3 get off. How many people are then left on the bus?

The correct answer is F. Please mark this in Practice Question 1 in the Problem Solving section of your answer sheet.

STOP AND WAIT FOR FURTHER INSTRUCTIONS

Several questions will follow for you to answer.

A £30	B £72	C 10	D 100	E £36
F 27	G £33	H £87	I £290	J £288

Select an answer to each question from the 10 different possible answers in the table above. You may use an answer for more than one question.

(1) Josie is planning her birthday party lunch. She is planning a trip to the local restaurant.

She invites 6 men and 5 women.

On the day of the party, $\frac{2}{3}$ of the invited men attend the party, and all of the women attend the party. They all choose the set menu at £29 per person.

How much was the total food bill?

(2) How many people are at the party in total?

(3) Josie has a discount voucher that gives 30% off the total food bill.

How much is the discount?

(4) The drinks totalled £85.

What was the total cost of the food and drink after the discount was deducted from the food?

(5) A tip of 12.5% was added to the bill as there were more than 6 people in the party.

What amount was the tip?

(6) If the total bill including tip is shared between all guests (excluding Josie as it is her birthday), how much should each guest pay?

(7) Alan and Diane are both guests at the party lunch. Alan has forgotten his money, so Diane offers to pay his share too.

How much does Diane pay?

CONTINUE WORKING

(8) Everyone sat down for lunch at 12:35, and the lunch finished at 14:15.

How long did the lunch last in minutes?

(9) The date of the birthday lunch is November 28th.

How many days are there until Christmas Day on December 25th?

(10) The party guests travel home in three separate taxis to different destinations.

The cost of the taxis was: £10.20, £8.30 and £11.50

A £1 tip was added on to each taxi cost.

What was the total paid for the taxis?

STOP AND WAIT FOR FURTHER INSTRUCTIONS ⊗

Antonyms

INSTRUCTIONS

 YOU HAVE 10 MINUTES TO COMPLETE THE FOLLOWING SECTION.

YOU HAVE 25 QUESTIONS TO COMPLETE WITHIN THE TIME GIVEN.

EXAMPLES

Example 1

Select the word that is least similar to the following word:

light

A	B	C	D	E
dark	water	feather	bright	hill

The correct answer is A. This has already been marked in Example 1 in the Antonyms section of your answer sheet.

Practice Question 1

Select the word that is least similar to the following word:

smooth

A	B	C	D	E
allow	beneath	rough	whilst	shade

The correct answer is C. Please mark the answer C in Practice Question 1 in the Antonyms section of your answer sheet.

STOP AND WAIT FOR FURTHER INSTRUCTIONS

In each row, select the word from the table that is least similar to the word above the table.

1 observe

A	B	C	D	E
seize	sparkle	overlook	operate	usual

2 nostalgic

A	B	C	D	E
float	unsentimental	fanatic	loathe	impress

3 decrepit

A	B	C	D	E
faulty	resume	dedicated	pristine	ineptitude

4 flavoursome

A	B	C	D	E
suppose	reunited	unpalatable	placated	somehow

5 develop

A	B	C	D	E
deter	deteriorate	decide	discount	return

6 maintain

A	B	C	D	E
nourish	congregate	extroverted	surge	neglect

CONTINUE WORKING ▶

7 glower

A	B	C	D	E
smirk	facilitate	shower	stentorian	dangle

8 punctual

A	B	C	D	E
digress	nimble	exterior	tardy	sturdy

9 prowess

A	B	C	D	E
adaptive	clumsiness	pride	rapturous	confess

10 brazen

A	B	C	D	E
timid	sledge	fast	sow	handsome

11 camouflage

A	B	C	D	E
evaluate	flask	vivid	dissuade	reveal

12 enchanting

A	B	C	D	E
prefer	dull	debt	meandering	immigrating

CONTINUE WORKING

13 glut

A	B	C	D	E
dearth	intestine	command	jocularity	infer

14 delectable

A	B	C	D	E
undetectable	horrid	palatial	apprehend	reason

15 gradual

A	B	C	D	E
establish	grade	disdain	rapid	bright

16 suspense

A	B	C	D	E
polite	feathered	certainty	clever	exhausted

17 modern

A	B	C	D	E
frequent	doubtful	despondent	ancient	diligent

18 former

A	B	C	D	E
benefit	current	seldom	quash	subtle

CONTINUE WORKING ⇨

19 full

A	B	C	D	E
upbeat	feigned	conscious	peckish	ripe

20 wound

A	B	C	D	E
round	lonely	straightened	squalid	typical

21 rigid

A	B	C	D	E
zealous	alike	true	flexible	elite

22 capacious

A	B	C	D	E
confined	below	necessary	hilarious	puny

23 flabbergasted

A	B	C	D	E
clammy	fragile	bustling	anxious	unimpressed

24 cause

A	B	C	D	E
stingy	prevent	tedious	capable	splendid

25 truth

A	B	C	D	E
heavenly	private	deceit	profuse	deceptive

STOP AND WAIT FOR FURTHER INSTRUCTIONS

Non-Verbal Reasoning

 YOU HAVE 8 MINUTES TO COMPLETE THE FOLLOWING SECTION.

YOU HAVE 15 QUESTIONS TO COMPLETE WITHIN THE TIME GIVEN.

EXAMPLES

CUBES Example 1

Look at the cube net.

Select the only cube that could be formed from the net.

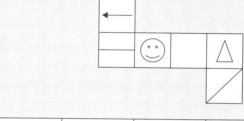

The correct answer is E. This has already been marked in Example 1 in the Non-Verbal Reasoning section of your answer sheet.

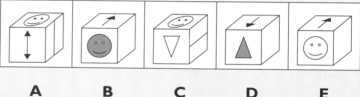

A   B   C   D   E

CUBES Practice Question 1

Look at the cube net.

Select the only cube that could be formed from the net.

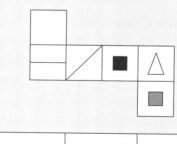

The correct answer is A. Please mark this in Practice Question 1 in the Non-Verbal Reasoning section of your answer sheet.

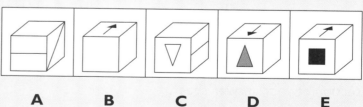

A   B   C   D   E

CONTINUE WORKING

REFLECTION Example 2

Select an image from the row that shows how the shape or pattern on the left will appear when reflected.

 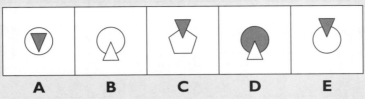

The correct answer is E. This has already been marked in Example 2 in the Non-Verbal Reasoning section of your answer sheet.

REFLECTION Practice Question 2

Select an image from the row that shows how the shape or pattern on the left will appear when reflected.

 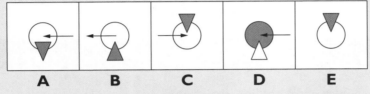

The correct answer is C. Please mark this in Practice Question 2 in the Non-Verbal Reasoning section of your answer sheet.

CODES Example 3

Look at the codes for the following patterns and identify the missing code for the pattern on the far right.

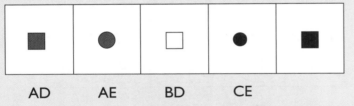

AD   AE   BD   CE

A	BE
B	AD
C	BC
D	BD
E	CD

The correct answer is E. This has already been marked in Example 3 in the Non-Verbal Reasoning section of your answer sheet.

CODES Practice Question 3

Look at the codes for the following patterns and identify the missing code for the pattern on the far right.

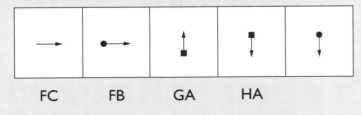

FC   FB   GA   HA

A	FA
B	GB
C	HB
D	HC
E	GC

The correct answer is C. Please mark this in Practice Question 3 in the Non-Verbal Reasoning section of your answer sheet.

STOP AND WAIT FOR FURTHER INSTRUCTIONS ✖

1. Look at the cube net. Select the only cube that could be formed from the net.

A   B   C   D   E

2. Look at the cube net. Select the only cube that could be formed from the net.

A   B   C   D   E

3. Look at the cube net. Select the only cube that could be formed from the net.

A   B   C   D   E

4. Look at the cube net. Select the only cube that could be formed from the net.

A   B   C   D   E

5. Look at the cube net. Select the only cube that could be formed from the net.

A   B   C   D   E

CONTINUE WORKING

6 Look at the codes for the following patterns and identify the missing code for the pattern on the far right.

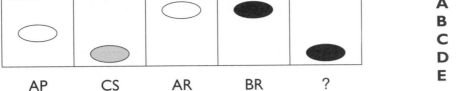

AP   CS   AR   BR   ?

A	BP
B	BR
C	BS
D	AS
E	DS

7 Look at the codes for the following patterns and identify the missing code for the pattern on the far right.

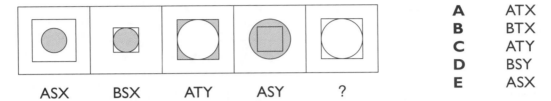

ASX   BSX   ATY   ASY   ?

A	ATX
B	BTX
C	ATY
D	BSY
E	ASX

8 Look at the codes for the following patterns and identify the missing code for the pattern on the far right.

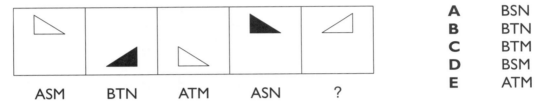

ASM   BTN   ATM   ASN   ?

A	BSN
B	BTN
C	BTM
D	BSM
E	ATM

9 Look at the codes for the following patterns and identify the missing code for the pattern on the far right.

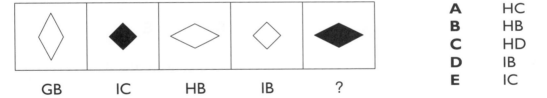

GB   IC   HB   IB   ?

A	HC
B	HB
C	HD
D	IB
E	IC

10 Look at the codes for the following patterns and identify the missing code for the pattern on the far right.

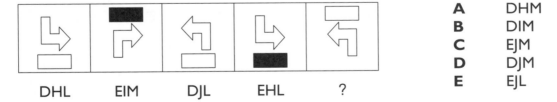

DHL   EIM   DJL   EHL   ?

A	DHM
B	DIM
C	EJM
D	DJM
E	EJL

CONTINUE WORKING ⇨

11 Look at the codes for the following patterns and identify the missing code for the pattern on the far right.

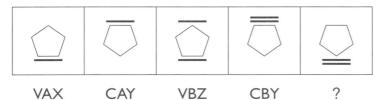

VAX   CAY   VBZ   CBY   ?

A   CAX
B   VBX
C   CBY
D   VBY
E   CBX

12 Select an image from the row below that shows how the shape or pattern on the left will appear when reflected.

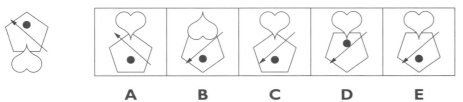

A   B   C   D   E

13 Select an image from the row below that shows how the shape or pattern on the left will appear when reflected.

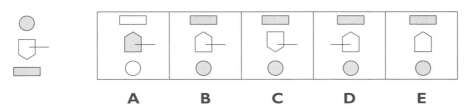

A   B   C   D   E

14 Select an image from the row below that shows how the shape or pattern on the left will appear when reflected.

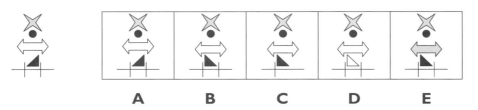

A   B   C   D   E

15 Select an image from the row below that shows how the shape or pattern on the left will appear when reflected.

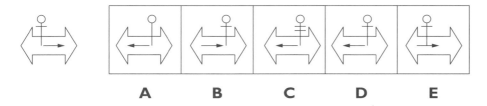

A   B   C   D   E

STOP AND WAIT FOR FURTHER INSTRUCTIONS ⊗

Shuffled Sentences

INSTRUCTIONS

 YOU HAVE 8 MINUTES TO COMPLETE THE FOLLOWING SECTION.

YOU HAVE 15 QUESTIONS TO COMPLETE WITHIN THE TIME GIVEN.

EXAMPLES

Example 1

The following sentence is shuffled and also contains one unnecessary word.
Rearrange the sentence correctly, in order to identify the unnecessary word.

dog the ran fetch the to stick gluing.

A	B	C	D	E
gluing	dog	ran	the	stick

The correct answer is A. This has already been marked in Example 1 in the Shuffled Sentences section of your answer sheet.

Practice Question 1

The following sentence is shuffled and also contains one unnecessary word.
Rearrange the sentence correctly, in order to identify the unnecessary word.

pushed Emma stood up and closed the table under the chairs.

A	B	C	D	E
chairs	stood	under	closed	Emma

The correct answer is D. Please mark this in Practice Question 1 in the Shuffled Sentences section of your answer sheet.

STOP AND WAIT FOR FURTHER INSTRUCTIONS

Each of the following sentences is shuffled and also contains one unnecessary word. Rearrange the sentence correctly, in order to identify the unnecessary word.

(1) going to a Holly Christmas shop to the tree buy went

A	B	C	D	E
Holly	a	going	tree	shop

(2) read some Edward has twice of his books ticket

A	B	C	D	E
some	read	his	ticket	Edward

(3) was it enough cold water to coat a need today

A	B	C	D	E
but	was	the	it	water

(4) now was the the up hill top becoming familiar route

A	B	C	D	E
the	top	familiar	up	was

(5) be table on the would dinner chairs soon

A	B	C	D	E
chairs	on	the	would	soon

(6) the rapids were in the rose river fierce it descended from the as mountains

A	B	C	D	E
the	rapids	river	rose	mountains

(7) though she was proud her in the of so exam achievement

A	B	C	D	E
of	proud	achievement	though	she

CONTINUE WORKING ⏵

8 twinkled the star Christmas houses on the the street glowed and with lights

A	B	C	D	E
the	star	lights	glowed	with

9 the premises record break is of a everyone who kept enters and leaves

A	B	C	D	E
break	kept	enters	leaves	is

10 the performers under stood the audience to cheer and applaud

A	B	C	D	E
stood	under	and	performers	audience

11 enjoyed the outside cycling the house where children

A	B	C	D	E
enjoyed	cycling	where	the	house

12 was it dark in run-up the hill to Christmas early so

A	B	C	D	E
dark	Christmas	so	hill	to

13 Christmas tree's about the evening twinkled and sparkled in the decorations

A	B	C	D	E
tree's	sparkled	about	the	in

14 open the lion roared as it the fire room heated

A	B	C	D	E
lion	fire	room	heated	as

CONTINUE WORKING

(15) some plant the seed in looked need water of

A	B	C	D	E
water	need	some	seed	the

END OF PAPER

THIS PAGE HAS DELIBERATELY BEEN LEFT BLANK

Answers to Test A, Paper 1

Comprehension

Q1 *E*
He has been evacuated from the city because of the war

Q2 *C*
She considered him a good role model for Billy

Q3 *B*
Billy had been kind; Edward didn't want to hurt Billy's feelings

Q4 *D*
A storm

Q5 *A*
It had disappeared

Q6 *E*
Adjective

Q7 *B*
Their daily household jobs

Q8 *D*
Delayed until later

Q9 *A*
They were afraid they wouldn't be allowed to continue exploring the garden

Q10 *A*
They took their coats and boots in case it rained

Shuffled Sentences

Note: Other sentences may be possible, leading to the same word being removed.

Q1 *A   fame*
She needed a photograph for her driving licence.

Q2 *B   depart*
There was a strong gust of wind and the leaves dispersed.

Q3 *E   aware*
The sign reminded guests to vacate their room by midday.

Q4 *B   accrued*
All customers with a loyalty card will receive a discount.

Q5 *D   take*
The children removed their shoes and paddled in the sea.

Q6 *C   excavation*
The bushes rustled as the rabbit retreated into the undergrowth.

Q7 *A   applaud*
The audience waited patiently for the show to start.

Q8 *E   sheath*
Although the knight fought bravely he could not defeat the dragon.

Q9 *D   scar*
The soldier had been seriously wounded in the battle.

Q10 *B   enhance*
After a gruelling trial the accused had been found guilty.

Q11 *A   inhibit*
He had been advised not to meddle with the equipment.

Q12 *E   they're*
In the end good will prevail over evil.

Q13 *D   entirety*
The glass fell from her hands and smashed on the floor.

Q14 *A   behaviour*
None of the puppies was given a name before being sold.

Q15 *B   resemble*
The dog ran off in pursuit of the cat.

Numeracy

Q1 *06*
This is the largest number that divides into both with no remainder.

Q2 *18*
70 × 3 = 210 eggs needed for 70 people (3 each)
18 × 12 = 216, so 18 boxes needed for 210 eggs

Q3 *25*
20 is 80% of the amount expected (20% fewer than expected), so 20 ÷ 4 x 5 = 25, which is 100% of those expected.

Q4 *09*
63 ÷ 7 = 9

Q5 *16*
Ben is 6 now, so Alan is 8 (6 + 2) and Jenny 16 (8 × 2)

Q6 *95*
The sequence is adding 1 then doubling.
94 + 1 = 95

Q7 78

Zero term would be 155 as sequence subtracts 7 for each new value. 11th term would be:

$155 - 7 \times 11 = 155 - 77 = 78$

Q8 07

24 pieces in total (2×12). Pieces eaten $= (2 \times 4) + (3 \times 3) = 8 + 9 = 17$, and so $24 - 17 = 7$

Q9 14

On March 26th this year I will be 13. I will become 14 on March 26th next year.

Q10 50

10 ml = 1 cl, so 500 ml = 50 cl

Q11 08

A cuboid is a box shape like a stretched cube.

Q12 23

Using BODMAS to determine the order of operations, the multiplication should be calculated before the addition, so $17 + 6 = 23$.

Q13 11

$4 + 7 = 11$

Problem Solving

Q1 E

Flight takes $7 + 1 = 8$ hours. Destination is 5 hours behind (2 p.m. $+ 7 + 1 - 5 = 5$ p.m.)

Q2 B

Janet cycles 8 km each hour (60 minutes), so 4 km in 30 minutes, or 2 km in 15 minutes.

Q3 D

There are two rectangles in the question: the area of the larger paving triangle surrounding the pond, and the pond itself. Subtracting the smaller from the larger will give the area of the path. Length of paving is $3 + 1 + 1 = 5$ m; width is $2 + 1 + 1 = 4$ m.
Subtraction of rectangle areas gives:
$(5 \times 4) - (3 \times 2) = 20 - 6 = 14$ m^2

Q4 A

Dividing the top and bottom of the fraction by 3 gives $\frac{5}{12}$

Q5 D

Interest for a year would be $10,000 \times 0.04 = £400$. So for half a year the interest would be half of that, £200.

Q6 D

A is not prime as divisible by 3; B is not under 15; C is even; E is even.

Q7 C

Not Blake or Edward as Ajay taller. Not Daniel as he is shorter than Blake and Colin. Colin taller than Ajay.

Q8 D

All sides equal length on a square. Perimeter is $4 \times$ length of the square's side, so $4 \times (t + 2)$ or $4(t + 2)$.

Q9 E

Each of the two diggers will dig 20 m^3 holes in 2 hours.

Q10 B

There are 9 spaces of 30 cm between the 10 steps. In addition, the ladder extends 30 cm below the bottom step and above the top step. So the height of the extended ladder is 11×30 cm = 330 cm = 3.3 m. When collapsed into a third of its size, it is $3.3 \div 3 = 1.1$ m

Synonyms

Q1 B gadget	**Q13** A evolve
Q2 C remember	**Q14** C naval
Q3 A courageous	**Q15** B smell
Q4 D usual	**Q16** D assign
Q5 C sorrow	**Q17** E tend
Q6 E perceptive	**Q18** C surpass
Q7 D celebratory	**Q19** B preference
Q8 C loaner	**Q20** C enclosed
Q9 D determine	**Q21** B brandish
Q10 A rude	**Q22** C lukewarm
Q11 C moisture	**Q23** D imaginative
Q12 B poisonous	**Q24** C long

Non-Verbal Reasoning

Q1 B

Number of non-bold lines increases from left to right and alternates from top to bottom.

Q2 D

Diamonds increase in number from left to right. The background colour and stripe direction alternates. Answer needs two white diamonds on a white background.

Q3 E

Every other image in the sequence is identical.

Q4 C

The inner shape rotates anti-clockwise as sequence progresses left to right, whilst outer square alternates from dashed to bold.

Q5 A

Q6 B

Q7 E

Q8 D

There are three of each shape in the grid (two grey and one white, which is inverted). Answer must be white pentagon pointing up.

Q9 C

Two white and one grey circle on each row, so one circle must be grey.

Q10 C

The middle row is a reflection in a vertical line of the top row. Alternatively, the middle row is a half turn rotation from the bottom row.

Q11 B

Three of the same images in the grid.

Q12 D

All images in diagonals are the same. Answer needs to be both grey and have a double ended arrow.

Q13 B

There are three of each shape in the grid; answer must be a triangle.

Answers to Test A, Paper 2

Problem Solving

Q1 B 51

13 days remain in May, plus 30 in June and 8 in July. 13 + 30 + 8 = 51

Q2 D 165

2 hours 45 minutes = 60 + 60 + 45 = 165

Q3 F 20

Ratio is 5 girls : 3 boys (from question)
If there are 12 boys then ratio scaled up by 4, so there are 5×4 girls = 20

Q4 C 600

8 adults × 30 = 240
8 children go free, so 32 − 8 = 24
24 children × 15 = 360
240 + 360 = 600

Q5 I 200

40 × 5 = 200

Q6 A 10

Last year May/June visitors = 67,600
This year May/June visitors = 60,840
Decrease is 6,760 which is $\frac{1}{10}$ or 10% of last year.

Q7 I 200

1 hectare = 10,000 m², so
2,000,000 ÷ 10,000 = 200

Q8 F 20

Went on 24 rides, i.e. 4 more rides than the 20 hoped.
$\frac{4}{20} = \frac{1}{5}$ = 20%

Q9 J 2045

Coach was 30 minutes quicker than the journey there, so 2 hours 45 less 30 minutes = 2 hours 15 minutes from 6.30 p.m. is 8.45 p.m. or 2045

Q10 H 110

Coach travels at 40 mph. Journey time is 2 hours 45 minutes.
40 miles in first hour, 40 miles in second hour, and in the remaining $\frac{3}{4}$ of an hour 30 miles travelled. So 40 + 40 + 30 = 110

Cloze

Q1	E	observation	Q11	D	highlights
Q2	H	formally	Q12	A	distinctly
Q3	A	formerly	Q13	J	appreciate
Q4	J	intended	Q14	G	fellow
Q5	F	capsules	Q15	E	knowledgeable
Q6	D	capacity	Q16	C	emergence
Q7	G	revolutions	Q17	H	invested
Q8	B	boarding	Q18	B	tapping
Q9	C	resembles	Q19	F	meandered
Q10	I	prominent	Q20	I	understand

Non-Verbal Reasoning

Q1 A

Half turn rotation

Q2 E

Quarter turn clockwise rotation

Q3 B

Half turn rotation

Q4 D

Half turn rotation

Q5 B
Quarter turn anti-clockwise rotation

Q6 C
Quarter turn anti-clockwise rotation

Q7 D
Half turn rotation

Q8 E
Quarter turn clockwise rotation

Q9 D
Middle row has no arrows; left and right columns point up.

Q10 C
Looking at each column from top to bottom, dots move around the squares in an anti-clockwise direction.

Q11 B
Looking at each row from left to right, dots move around squares clockwise.

Q12 D
Looking at each row from left to right, triangles rotate anti-clockwise, so blank must contain a triangle pointing up. Alternatively, looking at columns from top to bottom, triangles rotate clockwise.

Q13 B BY
Left letter represents shape (parallelogram is B), right letter represents the black rectangle being in the foreground or background (Y is background).

Q14 D CD
Left letter represents colour of middle star (black is C), right letter represents the colour of the bottom star (D is white) Note: colour of the top star does not relate to the code, which is why two different images can have same code.

Q15 C RYB
Left letter represents triangle pointing up or down (up is R), middle letter represents whether arrow points left or right (left being Y), and right letter represents the shape on the tail of the arrow (circle is B).

Grammar

Q1 E Wendesday
Correct spelling is Wednesday.

Q2 D adress
Correct spelling is address.

Q3 B desrition
Correct spelling is description.

Q4 C mis
Q5 B il
Q6 C always
Q7 E throughout
Q8 A luck

Antonyms

Q1 D injustice
Q2 E doubtful
Q3 E remember
Q4 B counterfeit
Q5 A secure
Q6 C endanger
Q7 E unspecified
Q8 D ignore
Q9 C elaborate
Q10 A variable
Q11 D sturdy
Q12 C random
Q13 B cheery
Q14 D agree
Q15 C withdrawn

Numeracy

Q1 06
Using BODMAS (as there are two operations), multiplication must be done before the addition.
$6 + (4 \times ?) = 30$, so $(4 \times ?)$ must be 24, so ? is 6
Note: single-digit numbers must be written using a '0' in the first column of the answer.

Q2 97
Each number is double the previous number minus 1.
$49 \times 2 = 98$. $98 - 1 = 97$
Alternatively, the difference between consecutive numbers in the sequence is doubling each time.
Differences are 3, 6, 12, 24, 48 and so $49 + 48 = 97$

Q3 27
10% of 30 is 3. $30 - 3 = 27$

Q4 15
$60 \div 4 = 15$
Chairs = 4 × number of tables, so tables = number of chairs ÷ 4

Q5 76
20 posts means 19 spaces between posts.
$19 \times 2 = 38$ m in length. Double this as two lengths of wire.

Q6 51
Aisha is 12 now. So Sheilesh is 17.
$17 + 34 = 51$

Q7 71
$48 + 49 + 12 - 12 - 37 - 12 + 23 = 71$

Q8 55
Film duration is $35 + 60 + 15 = 110$ minutes
$110 \div 2 = 55$

Q9 **B** 26

$5^2 = 25$, so $5^2 + 1 = 26$

Q10 **C** 3

$43 \div 5 = 8$ remainder 3

Q11 **C** 427

$1,972 - 862 - 683 = 427$

Q12 **C** 3

$110 \times 1.8 = 198$ which is the total number of people in the 110 occupied apartments. $198 - 195 = 3$

Q13 **C** 6

A cuboid is like a stretched cube.

Q14 **A** 1.04 kg

26×40 g $= 1,040$ g $= 1.04$ kg

Q15 **D** 5 coins

£2 coin, £1 coin, 20p, 20p, 2p

Q16 **C** 72°

Exterior angles on regular shape = $360° \div$ number of sides (5) = 72°

Q17 **E** 101

Two lampposts are needed for the first space of 20 m, and every additional lamppost will add another space of 20 m. There will always will one less space than lampposts (or to put it another way, one more lamppost than spaces). So, 2,000 m = 100 spaces of 20 m, which means there must be 101 lampposts.

Q18 **D** 14

In 4 years' time, Lara will be half of my mother's age then $(42 + 4) \div 2 = 23$, so Lara is now $23 - 4 = 19$ years old. I am 5 years younger than Lara, so $19 - 5 = 14$ years old (I will always be 5 years younger than Lara).

Answers to Test B, Paper 1

Comprehension

Q1 **E**

New housing development

Q2 **C**

Hampton

Q3 **C**

To the East

Q4 **B**

Verb

Q5 **B**

To really try to achieve the objective

Q6 **A**

Set up

Q7 **D**

Area of Outstanding Natural Beauty

Q8 **A**

Westhampton

Q9 **D**

The online gallery at www.blueridge/seaview/gallery.com

Q10 **B**

Malcolm Macintyre

Shuffled Sentences

Note: Other sentences may be possible, leading to the same word being removed.

Q1 **B** room

The showers will continue through the night.

Q2 **A** through

Jack thought that he may have forgotten his key.

Q3 **D** they

There were several options to choose from for lunch.

Q4 **E** hole

The new shelves were put to good use and nearly filled.

Q5 **C** careless

He weaved through the dense woodland being careful not to trample on the wildflowers.

Q6 **D** brought

The country lane meandered through the countryside.

Q7 **C** over

She struggled under the weight of the backpack.

Q8 **A** squid

The squalid living conditions were now no longer appropriate.

Q9 **D** reason

You will see this charming city at its best in summertime.

Q10 **B** departures

His arrival at the door was an unpleasant surprise.

Q11 **A** difference

This looked like the perfect spot for the picnic.

Q12 **D** *against*

It had been a long day and everyone was feeling weary.

Q13 **D** *clock*

It was about time he had some good luck.

Q14 **E** *average*

The train had become the most popular mode of transport in the city.

Q15 **A** *thunder*

The ambient lighting helped to create an atmosphere.

Numeracy

Q1 *02*

It is April 2nd (18 + 15 = 33). There are 31 days in March. 33 − 31 leaves 2 days, so April 2nd.

Q2 *04*

$52 \div (7 + 1) = 52 \div 8$

$6 \times 8 = 48$, so $52 - 48 = 4$ *remaining*

Q3 *12*

(5×2.4)

Q4 *01*

Walking at 3 miles per hour, means you are walking 1 mile every 20 minutes as there are 60 minutes in an hour.

Q5 *03*

Alan is 3 years older than Barry. If Alan is twice as old as Barry then Barry must be 3, and Alan 6.

Q6 *27*

There are two sequences within the sequence. The 1st, 3rd, 5th term, etc. are one sequence (which adds 3 each time) and the 2nd, 4th, 6th term, etc. is another sequence (which subtracts 2 each time).

Q7 *21*

Zero term would be 168 as sequence subtracts 7 for each new value. 21st term would be:

$168 - 7 \times 21 = 168 - 147 = 21$

Q8 *60*

Each weighs 480 g ÷ 8 = 60 g

4 out of 5 are disposed of. 1 piece remains, so 1 × 60 g = 60 g

Q9 *14*

There are 28 quarters in 7, so in half that there are 14.

Q10 *35*

10 mm = 1 cm, so 350 mm = 35 cm

Q11 *06*

Vertices are corners on 3D shapes, and an octahedron is diamond shaped, being one square based pyramid on top of another joining each other on the square faces.

Q12 *02*

Using BODMAS to determine the order of operations, the multiplication should be calculated before the subtraction, so 22 − 20 = 2.

Q13 *06*

$(7 \times 14) - (31 + 30 + 31) = 98 - 92 = 6$

Problem Solving

Q1 **G**

Each hour costs £16 for 2 adults, £8 for 2 children = £24 per hour. So 2 hours cost £48.

Q2 **A**

2 adult bikes cost £16 per hour, so £32 for 2 hours. 3 child bikes cost £12 per hour, £24 for 2 hours. So the cost before the family discount is £32 + £24 = £56. Discount is £56 − £50 = £6

Q3 **C**

12 km will take 1.5 hours at 8 km/h. Add in the 30-minute break, totals 2 hours or 120 minutes.

Q4 **D**

Family A are going half the speed of Family B. They set off in opposite directions around a circle. Family A will have completed one third of the route by the time Family B completes two thirds. This is the point at which they meet. A would have travelled 4 km, and B 8 km. For B to travel 8 km takes $\frac{2}{3}$ of an hour as they travel 12 km/h, so 40 minutes. Alternatively, Family A travels 4 km in $\frac{2}{3}$ of an hour as they travel at 6 km/h. They will meet after 40 minutes.

Q5 **E**

$0.05 \times 20{,}000 = 1{,}000$

$(0.05 = \frac{1}{20})$

Q6 **F**

$\frac{1}{3}$ *are child bikes and* $\frac{2}{3}$ *adult, so 48 ÷ 3 = 16 child and 32 adult*

Q7 **H**

32 adult bikes (see answer to Question 6)

£8 × 5 hours = £40 per bike per week

£40 × 32 = £1,280

Q8 I

£800 × 1.2 = £960

Q9 E

£12,000 ÷ 12 = £1,000

Q10 B

150 customers is 120% of last year's customers (from question)

150 ÷ 1.2 = 125 customers

Synonyms

Q1	**B**	*beginner*	**Q13**	**C**	*uncertainty*
Q2	**C**	*imminent*	**Q14**	**B**	*nautical*
Q3	**D**	*accidental*	**Q15**	**D**	*threatening*
Q4	**B**	*shallow*	**Q16**	**C**	*comparable*
Q5	**E**	*scanty*	**Q17**	**C**	*devoted*
Q6	**A**	*beginning*	**Q18**	**A**	*excessive*
Q7	**C**	*slip*	**Q19**	**D**	*divide*
Q8	**B**	*mysterious*	**Q20**	**B**	*smarten*
Q9	**C**	*declare*	**Q21**	**A**	*opening*
Q10	**A**	*gather*	**Q22**	**B**	*reject*
Q11	**B**	*confirm*	**Q23**	**D**	*plentiful*
Q12	**D**	*stroll*			

Non-Verbal Reasoning

Q1 C

Black dots decreasing in number whilst grey dots are increasing from left to right; need four grey and one black for the answer.

Q2 C

Total number of sides is increasing from left to right; need six sides for the answer.

Q3 B

Thick black arrow which remains in bottom right is rotating clockwise as the sequence moves from left to right. Other arrow must be double-headed (one each end).

Q4 D

The three overlapping shapes alter their position foreground/middle/background as sequence progresses right to left. Triangle should be in middle, pentagon in background, square in foreground. Floating shape is a trapezium.

Q5 A

Number of crossovers is increasing from left to right. Need five crossovers for the answer.

Q6 C

Arrows alternate pointing left and right. Position alters from top to middle to bottom, to middle, so top next. Answer needs to be arrow pointing left at the top.

Q7 E

Grey circle position alters from top to middle to bottom, to middle, so top next. Square is big, medium, small then big, so medium next. Medium square with circle at the top of the image is the answer.

Q8 B

Number of sides reduces by one from left to right, starting at 8, 7, 6, ?, 4, so answer must have five sides.

Q9 D

Triangles rotate anti-clockwise, whilst black cross rotates clockwise as sequence progresses from left to right.

Q10 B

White triangles rotate anti-clockwise as sequence moves from left to right, whilst the black triangle moves from bottom to middle to top then back down. Answer needs black triangle in middle, and white in bottom left.

Q11 B

As sequence progresses from left to right, number of circles increases by one each time, and the circle colour alternates between black and grey, and face is reflected in horizontal line to the top of the space. When face at the bottom there is also a black arc above. Answer needs three black dots, face at bottom with arc above face.

Q12 C

White dots are on a diagonal loop from top left to bottom right then middle and so on. Black dots move from right to left in middle of the space as the sequence moves from left to right. Answer needs white dot top left and black dot right.

Q13 B

As sequence progresses from right to left, background colour alternates from black to grey, and inner rectangle alternates from grey to white. The stripes within each black outlined rectangle alternate from horizontal to vertical. So the missing image in the sequence must have a black outlined rectangle, with a grey inner rectangle having horizontal stripes.

Q14 B

Pair of arrows is rotating around the space anti-clockwise, whilst the black and white arrows swap places each time. Answer needs arrows on right of the space, pointing down, with the black arrow on the inside.

Answers to Test B, Paper 2

Problem Solving

Q1 G 70
£14 = 20%, so 100% is the price before the discount
5 × 20% = 100%, so 5 × £14 = £70

Q2 G 70
2 adult tickets cost the same as 4 child tickets, so 2 adult and 3 children's tickets are the same as 7 child tickets @ £10 each = £70

Q3 D 64
80 is 25% more than last year. If last year was 100%, then this year is 125%.
To get from 125% to 100%, divide by 5 then multiply by 4.
80 ÷ 5 = 16
16 × 4 = 64

Q4 A 75
He is cycling at 30 km per hour. So in 2 hours he travels 60 km, and in the half hour he travels $\frac{1}{2}$ of 30 = 15 km
In the 2.5 hours he travels
60 + 15 = 75 km

Q5 D 64
Area of trapezium is average length of the 2 parallel sides × distance between the parallel sides
Average of parallel sides is (10 + 6) ÷ 2 = 8
8 × 8 = 64

Q6 H 1,500
To convert at that rate from $ to £, ÷ 5 × 4, so, 1,875 ÷ 5 = 375
375 × 4 = 1,500

Q7 G 70
91 ÷ 1.3 is the same as (910 ÷ 13)
910 ÷ 13 = 70

Q8 D 64
Multiplying the times by 1,000 will convert them into thousandths, so:
12,668 − 12,604 = 64

Q9 J 1,084
864 + 235 − 15 = 1,084

Q10 E 53
June 4th to July 26th
30 days in June

30 − 4 = 26, plus the 4th itself, so 27 (question says inclusive of first and last day)
Add to this the 26 days in July:
27 + 26 = 53

Cloze

Q1	**H** lethargic	**Q11**	**I** browsed
Q2	**J** hallucinating	**Q12**	**G** aisles
Q3	**G** reluctantly	**Q13**	**E** croissants
Q4	**A** packaging	**Q14**	**D** ornately
Q5	**C** horrible	**Q15**	**H** toppers
Q6	**I** startled	**Q16**	**F** choose
Q7	**E** looming	**Q17**	**J** thought
Q8	**D** willing	**Q18**	**A** disgusting
Q9	**B** proud	**Q19**	**B** particular
Q10	**F** environment	**Q20**	**C** dissatisfied

Non-Verbal Reasoning

Q1 E
Only answer with an arrowhead on each end.

Q2 E
Only answer without rounded corners on the outer shape.

Q3 C
Only answer where the stacked shapes have two right angles at the bottom rather than the top as they are on other answer options.

Q4 C
Only answer where the shape in the foreground overlaps on the curve rather than the straight edge of the shape in the background.

Q5 C
Only answer where the number of sides on the inner shape is not one less than the number of sides on the outer shape (both have 6 on option C).

Q6 B
Only image where there are two white circles rather than one.

Q7 C
Net requires half turn rotation.

Q8 D
No rotation of net required.

Q9 B
No rotation of net required.

Q10 *B*

No rotation of net required.

Q11 *A*

No rotation of net required.

Q12 *D*

No rotation of net required.

Q13 *A*

No rotation of net required. Note that the cube cannot have two blank faces as they will be opposite faces from the net; also it is not possible to have three lines as there are two pairs of opposite faces with lines on the net. It is only possible to form a cube that has one of each pairs of lines that are on opposite faces, so two lines maximum.

Antonyms

Q1 *D cheery*

Q2 *C apprehension*

Q3 *E infrequency*

Q4 *B enhance*

Q5 *D overlook*

Q6 *A welcome*

Q7 *B preference*

Q8 *C reluctance*

Q9 *D anonymous*

Q10 *B substantial*

Q11 *B sound*

Q12 *C dishonest*

Q13 *E interesting*

Q14 *A attentive*

Q15 *B lengthy*

Numeracy

Q1 *36*

$(2 \times 60) - (12 \times 7) = 120 - 84$

Q2 *06*

Using BODMAS, $2 + (3 \times ?) = 20$, so $3 \times ?$ must $= 18$ because $2 + 18 = 20$, so $? = 6$

Q3 *16*

Difference between each pair of consecutive numbers is 1, 2, 3, 4, so next number is 5 more than the last number in the sequence, $11 + 5 = 16$

Q4 *02*

18 is 2 more than 16, so 16 is 8 times this number, so the number must be $16 \div 8 = 2$

Q5 *12*

Everyone in the 'Long hair' set that is not also in the 'Brown hair' set, so $7 + 5 = 12$

Q6 *20*

The sum of everyone outside the 'Blonde hair' set (including the 3 children who do not have long hair, brown hair or blonde hair), so $7 + 4 + 6 + 3 = 20$

Q7 *12*

$27 \div (5 + 4) = 3$ *groups of 5 boys and 4 girls in the class, so $3 \times 4 = 12$ girls*

Q8 *16*

I am 9 now, so was 8 a year ago. My brother is now $2 \times 8 = 16$

Q9 *£80*

£60 is 75% of the cost before the discount. To get back to the cost before the discount (100%), divide by 3 and multiply by 4 (i.e. $75 \div 3 \times 4 = 100$). So, $£60 \div 3 = £20$, $£20 \times 4 = £80$

Q10 *10*

Adding a to both sides gives: $40 = 4a$, $a = 10$

Q11 *51*

6 days left in May

June 30 days, 15 days to July 15th, so $6 + 30 + 15 = 51$

Q12 *06*

$42 \div (6 + 1) = 6$ *(remember to include myself)*

Q13 *05*

If everyone has one piece then the 2 cakes have been cut into 15 pieces each, so 30 pieces in total. If $\frac{1}{6}$ of the 30 pieces remain, that is $30 \div 6 = 5$ pieces remain

Q14 *30*

For every sweet Jan has, Jack has 3, and Bob 6. So for every 10 sweets the ratio is $1 : 3 : 6$ for Jan, Jack and Bob. There are 50 sweets in total. Multiplying the ratio by 5 gives the total sweets each: 5, 15, 30.

Q15 *05*

£1 coin, 50p, 20p, 5p, 1p

Q16 *29*

$(8 + 21)$

Q17 *21*

2 lampposts are needed for the first space of 50 m, and every additional lamppost will add another space of 50 m. There will always will one less space than lampposts (or to put it another way, one more lamppost than spaces). So, 1,000 m = 20 spaces of 50 m, which means there must be 21 lampposts.

Q18 *14*

In 4 years' time, Lucy will be $(40 + 4) \div 2 = 22$, so Lucy is now $22 - 4 = 18$ years old. I am 4 years younger than Lucy, so $18 - 4 = 14$ years old (I will always be 4 years younger than Lucy).

Answers to Test C, Paper 1

Comprehension

Q1 D
Edward has been to St Ives at least five times already

Q2 C
Three sisters

Q3 D
220 miles

Q4 E
In a castle converted into a railway hotel

Q5 D
10–12 guests

Q6 C
Verb

Q7 C
Large leaves on a tropical plant

Q8 D
Adjective

Q9 A
Searching the rock pools for crabs and small fish

Q10 D
The uphill walk back to the hotel after a day out

Grammar

Q1 C
'who's' should be 'whose'

Q2 A
'Me and Sam' should be 'Sam and I'

Q3 A
'It's' should be 'Its'

Q4 D
'piece of mind' should be 'peace of mind'

Q5 C
'expresso' should be 'espresso'

Q6 C
'would of' should be 'would have'

Q7 B
'isn't nobody' should be 'isn't anybody'

Q8 A
'effected me' should be 'affected me'

Q9 E
No errors

Numeracy

Q1 C 6
Triangle is equilateral as all angles are 60°.
3 × 2 cm = 6 cm

Q2 E 2
It will look identical after a half turn rotation.

Q3 A 6
Connecting opposite corners via the centre dividing it in half each time produces six equilateral triangles

Q4 B 16
Area of triangle is half × base × height, so half × base (4) × 16 = 32

Q5 C 2
As 1 m² = 100 cm × 100 cm = 10,000 cm²

Q6 A 85
From left to right the difference between consecutive numbers reduces by 1 (11, 10, 9, 8, 7).

Q7 B 24
10% of 120 is 12, so 20% is 24.

Q8 E 24
36 ÷ 3 × 2 = 24

Q9 D 36
Today I am 15, and so my brother must be 12 as he is 3 years younger than me.
12 × 3 = 36

Q10 B 45°
360 ÷ 8 = 45°

Q11 A 4
A triangular based pyramid.

Q12 D 4
(a + 1) must be 5, so a is 4.

Q13 C 14
If the mean of four numbers is 14, then the total must be 14 × 4 = 56. Subtracting the three numbers we know from the question (12, 16 and 14) leaves 14.

Q14 B 476

Q15 C 3.2642
Move the decimal point two columns to the left.

Q16 A 49
Also 7³ is 343, so dividing by 7 is 7² = 49

Q17 E 3 mph
1.5 miles in half an hour means I will travel 3 miles in an hour, so 3 mph.

Q18 E 10.0101

Q19 B 21.101

Q20 **D** £2.23

As $3.99 + 1.75 + 1.49 - 5 = 2.23$

Q21 **A** 4, 2, 8, 7

$4,885 - 2,677 = 2,208$

Q22 **C** 7, 0, 6, 8

$7,638 + 1,363 = 9,001$

Q23 **C** north-east

Q24 **A** 62

Q25 **D** 941

Q26 **B** 35.2

As $1\% = 0.8$, so $4\% = 3.2$, and $10\% = 8$, so $40\% = 32$

Therefore $44\% = 32 + 3.2 = 35.2$

Q27 **D** 1.35 p.m.

2 hours 15 minutes before 3.50 p.m.

Q28 **C** 120,000 cm^3

$60 \times 40 \times 50$

Q29 **B** 13

Q30 **C** 3, 8, 1, 2, 7

Sum of rows, columns and diagonals of 3 is 15 $(4 + 5 + 6)$

Q31 **A** 3,750 days

$15,000 \div 4 = 3,750$ days

Q32 **C** 2,152

Q33 **A** 92 km

As each dog walks 2×500 m $= 1$ km, so 92×1 km

Q34 **D** 0.15

Q35 **D** 2.75

Q36 **E** 50

Special offer box of 60 chocolates is 120% of the standard box.

$60 \div 6 \times 5 = 50$ chocolates in the standard box

Q37 **B** £50

£40 is 80% of the pocket money, so 100% of my pocket money would be $£40 \div 8 \times 10 = £50$

Q38 **C** 21 hours

Robot is on for $1.5 \times 2 = 3$ hours each day, so 21 hours per week.

Q39 **D** −9° Celsius

$-1 - 8 = -9$

Synonyms

Q1 **D** signal

Q2 **C** devoted

Q3 **A** related

Q4 **B** hidden

Q5 **A** purpose

Q6 **E** sumptuous

Q7 **C** ambitious

Q8 **B** different

Q9 **A** agreement

Q10 **C** lifestyle

Q11 **C** reviewed

Q12 **C** perfume

Q13 **B** reject

Q14 **B** likely

Q15 **A** rush

Q16 **A** muggy

Q17 **D** investigate

Q18 **A** beaten

Q19 **A** abundant

Q20 **C** secret

Non-Verbal Reasoning

Q1 **D**

This is a quarter turn anti-clockwise rotation of the original image.

Q2 **D**

This is a quarter turn anti-clockwise rotation of the original image.

Q3 **A**

This is a half turn rotation of the original image.

Q4 **E**

This is a quarter turn clockwise rotation of the original image.

Q5 **D**

This is a 135° turn anti-clockwise rotation of the original image.

Q6 **E**

This is a quarter turn clockwise rotation of the original image. Note on 'A' the line has moved position on the background shape.

Q7 **B**

Horizontal integration of right column over left column to form middle.

Q8 **A**

Horizontal integration of left column over middle column to form right.

Q9 **B**

The only answer where there is a grey circle (as there is one on each row).

Q10 **A**

Rotation of top row 90° clockwise to make bottom row from top.

Q11 **D**

The shapes in the corners are rotating anti-clockwise as you move in that direction around the grid.

Q12 **C**

In each row from left to right, the black circle moves clockwise around the set of four circles within each square of the grid.

Q13 **D**

Rotation of the left column by 45° clockwise gives the right column.

Answers to Test C, Paper 2

Cloze Sentences

Q1 *E about, sister's*
He was so excited about seeing his sister's new puppy after school.

Q2 *C evidence, conclusion*
Based on the evidence, he came to the conclusion that it was indeed the right thing to do.

Q3 *B its, evolved*
Throughout history, its meaning has evolved as language adapted to society.

Q4 *D privilege, present*
It is a great privilege to have been asked to present this special bravery award to you.

Q5 *A forward, on*
She was very much looking forward to taking in the sunshine on a pleasant stroll through the countryside this afternoon.

Q6 *C lessons, learned*
Many lessons had been learned as a result of her recent experiences.

Q7 *E children's, their*
The children's application of their knowledge was being tested in this week's quiz.

Q8 *A seldom, dark*
He seldom went out on his bike as it was almost dark when he arrived home from school during the winter months.

Q9 *C accept, our*
Please accept our apologies for not arriving on time.

Q10 *B especially, to*
Sam is especially looking forward to the start of the half-term holidays, as it will be the first time he has been camping.

Q11 *one*
The game was postponed until a later date.

Q12 *met*
Sometimes they had dinner a bit later on Fridays.

Q13 *end*
Jack's parents were tremendously proud of what he had achieved.

Q14 *raw*
The boy was described as unkempt and rather scrawny.

Q15 *pit*
The hosts had been particularly hospitable towards their guests.

Q16 *van*
You would have to have been particularly observant to have noticed that.

Q17 *tan (or ant)*
The new neighbour's children became friends instantly with other local youngsters.

Problem Solving

Q1 *J* 260
$£60 \times 4\frac{1}{3} = 240 + 20 = £260$

Q2 *G* 20
Rosa can afford to spend £60. This is after the discount, so is 75% of the full cost of £80.
She saves £20 each week.

Q3 *D* 54
Rosa's discount is £18 which is 25% of the full cost of the shopping which must have been $4 \times 18 = £72$, so the discounted cost is 75% of 72 = $18 \times 3 = £54$

Q4 *C* 52
She has a coffee every other week.
52 weeks ÷ 2 = 26
$26 \times £2 = £52$

Q5 *A* 14
The twins' birthday of December 24th + 7 days to the end of the year, then 14 days in January (7 + 14 = 21 which is the age difference in days). So Rosa's birthday is the 14th day of January.

Q6 *H* 32
3 yoghurts now cost the price of 2 so $48p \times 2 = 96p$, so 32 pence each.

Q7 *I* 50
The offer reduces the cost from 48p to 32p. Rosa then gets 25% off the offer cost of 32p, so $32 \times 75\% = 24p$. Overall a discount from 48p to 24p, which is 50%

Q8 *F* 10
1 hour 45 minutes after 9.25 a.m. is 11.10 a.m.

Q9 *F* 10
Rosa cycles 1 mile in 6 minutes which is the same as 10 miles in 60 minutes, or 10 miles per hour.

Q10 *E 1,175*

Rosa works 47 weeks as she has 5 weeks off each year. $47 \times 25 = 1{,}175$ hours

Antonyms

Q1 *E delightful*

Q2 *B scarce*

Q3 *A protected*

Q4 *C fight*

Q5 *D neglect*

Q6 *B clumsiness*

Q7 *C introverted*

Q8 *A indulge*

Q9 *C disobedient*

Q10 *B disputed*

Q11 *A contemporary*

Q12 *D curt*

Q13 *B incidental*

Q14 *C innovative*

Q15 *A fading*

Q16 *D deter*

Q17 *E minor*

Q18 *D rational*

Q19 *B prudence*

Q20 *A assistance*

Q21 *B inexperienced*

Q22 *C danger*

Q23 *B indifferent*

Q24 *E mute*

Q25 *D frosty*

Non-Verbal Reasoning

Q1 *C*

Black circle moves clockwise as you move from left to right on the rows of the grid. Grey circles move anti-clockwise as you move from left to right on the rows of the grid. Black and grey circles are always on the same row.

Q2 *B*

Top row reflected vertically to form bottom row.

Q3 *C*

Reflection in a diagonal line on grid from bottom left up to top right.

Q4 *B*

Each row has an arrow in the top, middle and bottom position of each individual square within the grid. Arrows in middle column face left.

Q5 *A*

Rotation of the image a quarter turn anti-clockwise.

Q6 *B*

Rotation of the image a quarter turn clockwise.

Q7 *A*

Rotation of the image a quarter turn anti-clockwise.

Q8 *B*

Rotation of the image by a half turn.

Q9 *A*

Reflection in a horizontal line.

Q10 *A*

Reflection in a horizontal line.

Q11 *B*

Reflection in a vertical line.

Q12 *D*

Reflection in a horizontal line.

Q13 *E*

Reflection in a horizontal line.

Q14 *C*

Black dots increase as sequence moves from left to right. Pentagon colour and arrow position and direction alternate too.

Q15 *E*

Moving from right to left, the face rotates clockwise a quarter turn each time. In addition, the star moves anti-clockwise moving from right to left.

Shuffled Sentences

Note: Other sentences may be possible, leading to the same word being removed.

Q1 *B given*

The farmer gave money to the poor because he was rich.

Q2 *A roll*

The role of a baker is to bake bread.

Q3 *D petal*

She rose from her comfortable garden seat to water the plants.

Q4 *C wear*

Name labels must be sewn onto all items of uniform.

Q5 *B passed*

She had spent the past six months attempting to pass her driving test.

Q6 *D paper*

The present that she had unwrapped brought a tear to her eye.

Q7 *E blow*

The wind section of the orchestra was out of tune.

Q8 *B hole*

She couldn't get in because she had lost her key.

Q9 *C telescope*

The stars shone like diamonds in the night sky.

Q10 *A road*

It is illegal to drive a car without a licence.

Q11 *E* *juice*
He tried to squeeze everything into the suitcase.

Q12 *B* *strawberry*
I spent the afternoon stuck in a traffic jam.

Q13 *D* *she*
Her rudeness could no longer be tolerated.

Q14 *D* *released*
His usual train was busy so he caught the next one.

Q15 *C* *knife*
They followed the signs until they came to a fork in the road.

Answers to Test D, Paper 1

Comprehension

Q1 *A*
An area where dangerous garden equipment is stored safely out of the children's reach

Q2 *B*
Anxious

Q3 *D*
Without adult supervision the children will do what they like

Q4 *E*
She was intrigued by the mystery

Q5 *D*
To demonstrate obsessive behaviour

Q6 *A*
His negativity was spoiling her fun

Q7 *E*
She reminded him that, if found out, he would be in as much trouble as her

Q8 *A*
Abstract noun

Q9 *D*
You have to accept the consequences of your actions

Q10 *C*
She realised how much trouble she would be in if discovered

Q11 *A*
Ellie had been ill recently and Norman was supposed to be supporting her through a difficult time

Q12 *B*
Involved in some wrongdoing along with others

Q13 *C*
guilt

Q14 *A*
Confessed to having been in the prohibited area of the garage and trying to open the trunk

Numeracy

Q1 *A* *11*
Substitute information in the question:
$a = 5$, so $2a + 1 = 2 \times 5 + 1 = 11$

Q2 *A* *9*
$25 - 16 = 9$

Q3 *B* *22*
$176 \div 8 = 22$

Q4 *B* *120 degrees*
interior + exterior = 180 degrees
exterior = 360 ÷ 6 (number of sides)
= 60 degrees
interior = 180 − 60 = 120 degrees

Q5 *E* *10*
Substitute information in the question:
If $b = 2a − 4$, and $b = 16$, then $16 = 2a − 4$
So adding 4 to both sides, $20 = 2a$, and so $a = 10$

Q6 *A* *0.5*
Substitute information in the question:
$12a − b = 0$, and $b = 6$, so $12a − 6 = 0$
Adding 6 to both sides gives $12a = 6$, so $a = 0.5$

Q7 *C* *16*
Multiplication operation before addition (using BODMAS) so $16 + ? = 32$, $? = 16$

Q8 *B* *4*
Division before addition using BODMAS, so $4 + (8 \div ?) = 6$, $4 + 2 = 6$, so $8 \div ? = 2$, $? = 4$

Q9 *E* *30*
Multiplication operation before addition (using BODMAS), so $? + 10 = 40$, $? = 30$

Q10 *C* *2*
Each roll costs $£2.50 \times 3 = £7.50$
For £15, I can buy 2 rolls as $2 \times £7.50 = £15$

Q11 *A* *1 in 2*
Each toss of the coin has a probability of 1 in 2 of getting a head or a tail.

Q12 *B* 4

$7 + 8 - 11 = 4$

Q13 *A* 21

$49 ÷ 7 = 7, 7 × 3 = 21$

Q14 *C* 18

From left to right, every other number in the sequence is 2 higher than the previous.

Q15 *A* 12

Isla is 7 (from question), so Rosa is $7 - 5 = 2$. So Edward is $2 × 5 = 10$, and Holly is then $10 + 2 = 12$

Q16 *C* 6

$42 ÷ 7$ (i.e. $6 + 1$) $= 6$ (must include me)

Q17 *B* 18

There are 30 minutes from 7.30 a.m. until I arrive at 8 a.m. The lowest common multiple of 8 and 12 (over 30) is 48. 48 minutes after 7.30 a.m. is 8.18 a.m., so 18 minutes wait after 8 a.m.

Q18 *D* 26

This is two sequences in one, or an alternating sequence. The 2nd, 4th, 6th numbers being 17, 20, 23 so a step or difference of +3 each time.

Q19 *E* one third of 40

In order of answers: 62, 14, 14.2, 13.5, 13.3̇

Q20 *C* 19

$15 - 3 + 7 = 19$

Q21 *E* 6

Range is highest less the lowest $= 9 - 3 = 6$

Q22 *A* 5.75

Mean is the sum of the data, divided by the number of pieces of data $= 46 ÷ 8 = 5.75$

Q23 *C* 5.5

Find middle data value when arranged in size order:

3, 4, 4, 5, 6, 7, 8, 9 so halfway between 5 and 6 (there are two pieces of data in the middle as there is an even number (8) of data), which is 5.5

Q24 *A* 18

There are 10 pieces of data, so arranging them in order of size, the middle is halfway between 18 and 18, which is 18.

Q25 *C* 18

Mode is most often occurring piece of data.

Q26 *A* 17

Mean is the sum of the data, divided by the number of pieces of data.

$170 ÷ 10 = 17$

Q27 *B* 30

Range is highest value minus the lowest value. $32 - 2 = 30$

Q28 *D* Ibraheem and Saket

$29 + 32 = 61$

Synonyms

Q1 *C* shy
Q2 *D* hate
Q3 *C* periodic
Q4 *E* conceited
Q5 *B* remember
Q6 *A* height
Q7 *B* peak
Q8 *D* adventurous
Q9 *A* boring
Q10 *D* shared
Q11 *C* unbelievable
Q12 *D* divided
Q13 *B* review
Q14 *E* depicted
Q15 *C* act
Q16 *A* symbol
Q17 *E* bewildered
Q18 *D* earlier
Q19 *B* loving
Q20 *A* excess

Non-Verbal Reasoning

Q1 *E*

This is a quarter turn clockwise of the original image.

Q2 *B*

This is a half turn of the original image.

Q3 *E*

The only answer where there is no square.

Q4 *B*

The only answer where there is no grey shaded shape.

Q5 *B*

The only answer where the arrow points down to the left.

Q6 *B*

The only answer where there is no heart shape.

Q7 *E*

The only answer where there are no stripes.

Q8 *E*

The only answer where there are two of the same shape.

Q9 *D*

The only answer where there is not a triangle in the foreground.

Q10 *C*

The arrows with grey cylinders should point right.

Q11 *A*

The only answer where the corner is turned up on the bottom left.

Q12 *E*

The only answer where the black dot is large.

Q13 A
Reflection in a vertical line.
Q14 B
Reflection in a vertical line.

Q15 C
Reflection in a vertical line.

Answers to Test D, Paper 2

Cloze Sentences

Q1 H *emphatic*
Q2 F *affability*
Q3 B *obdurate*
Q4 E *defunct*
Q5 J *nostalgia*

Q6 G *disdain*
Q7 D *irritable*
Q8 A *laceration*
Q9 C *intricate*
Q10 I *toil*

Q11 led
The shoppers jost**led** as they eagerly searched for bargains in the bustling shop.

Q12 end
Sarah was happy l**end**ing her pen to Jack as long as he returned it.

Q13 era
The regen**era**tion of the town centre by the local authority was long overdue.

Q14 tin
Her school teachers had always known Ella was des**tin**ed for great things.

Q15 ten
Andy thought the new boy to join the class was rather pre**ten**tious.

Q16 ran
The new b**ran**ch of the business had been established during the recent turbulent times.

Q17 tin
For a flee**tin**g moment I saw a rabbit up ahead among the trees.

Problem Solving

Q1 I *£290*
$\frac{2}{3}$ of 6 = 4
(4 + 5) × £29 = £261
Add in the cost of Josie's meal:
£29 + £261 = £290

Q2 C *10*
$\frac{2}{3}$ of 6 = 4 men, 5 women invited plus Josie

Q3 H *£87*
$\frac{3}{10}$ of 290
29 × 3 = £87

Q4 J *£288*
Food less discount = £290 − £87 = £203
Drink = £85
Total = £203 + £85 = £288

Q5 E *£36*
12.5% = $\frac{1}{8}$, so 288 ÷ 8 = £36

Q6 E *£36*
Total bill including tip is £288 + £36 = £324
Total guests (exclude Josie, per question)
10 − 1 = 9
Each pays £324 ÷ 9 = £36

Q7 B *£72*
Diane pays for herself and Alan so
£36 × 2 = £72

Q8 D *100*
Add on 2 hours (120 minutes) to start time, then subtract 20 minutes gives 100 minutes.

Q9 F *27*
2 days left in November (which has 30 days) plus 25 days in December until Christmas Day (December 25th).

Q10 G *£33*
Total cost of three taxis is
£30 plus 3 × £1 tips = £33

Antonyms

Q1 C *overlook*
Q2 B *unsentimental*
Q3 D *pristine*
Q4 C *unpalatable*
Q5 B *deteriorate*
Q6 E *neglect*
Q7 A *smirk*
Q8 D *tardy*
Q9 B *clumsiness*
Q10 A *timid*
Q11 E *reveal*
Q12 B *dull*
Q13 A *dearth*

Q14 B *horrid*
Q15 D *rapid*
Q16 C *certainty*
Q17 D *ancient*
Q18 B *current*
Q19 D *peckish*
Q20 C *straightened*
Q21 D *flexible*
Q22 A *confined*
Q23 E *unimpressed*
Q24 B *prevent*
Q25 C *deceit*

Non-Verbal Reasoning

Q1 *B*
No rotation of net required.

Q2 *D*
Net requires half turn rotation.

Q3 *D*
Net requires half turn rotation.

Q4 *D*
Net requires quarter turn rotation anti-clockwise.

Q5 *E*
Net requires half turn rotation.

Q6 *C BS*
The first letter relates to the colour. The second letter relates to the position of the shape.

Q7 *A ATX*
The first letter relates to the size of the outer shape (big or small). The second letter relates to the colour of the inner shape. The third letter relates to the colour of the outer shape.

Q8 *D BSM*
The first letter relates to the right angle being on the left or right of the triangle. The second letter relates to the position of the triangle (top or bottom). The third letter relates to triangle colour.

Q9 *A HC*
The first letter relates to shape and orientation. The second letter relates to colour.

Q10 *D DJM*
The first letter relates to the colour of the rectangle. The second letter relates to the orientation of the arrow. The third letter relates to the position of the rectangle (top/bottom).

Q11 *E CBX*
The first letter relates to the orientation of the pentagon. The second letter relates to the number of floating lines. The third letter relates to the position of the floating lines (top/bottom/both).

Q12 *E*
Reflection in a horizontal line above or below the image.

Q13 *B*
Reflection in a horizontal line above or below the image.

Q14 *B*
Reflection in a vertical line to the left or right of the image.

Q15 *D*
Reflection in a vertical line to the left or right of the image.

Shuffled Sentences

Note: Other sentences may be possible, leading to the same word being removed.

Q1 *C going*
Holly went to the shop to buy a Christmas tree.

Q2 *D ticket*
Edward has read some of his books twice.

Q3 *E water*
It was cold enough to need a coat today.

Q4 *B top*
The route up the hill was now becoming familiar.

Q5 *A chairs*
Dinner would be on the table soon.

Q6 *D rose*
The rapids in the river were fierce as it descended from the mountains.

Q7 *D though*
She was so proud of her achievement in the exam.

Q8 *B star*
The houses on the street glowed and twinkled with the Christmas lights.

Q9 *A break*
A record is kept of everyone who enters and leaves the premises.

Q10 *B under*
The audience stood to cheer and applaud the performers.

Q11 *C where*
The children enjoyed cycling outside the house.

Q12 *D hill*
It was dark so early in the run-up to Christmas.

Q13 *C about*
The Christmas tree's decorations sparkled and twinkled in the evening.

Q14 *A lion*
The open fire roared as it heated the room.

Q15 *D seed*
The plant looked in need of some water.

THIS PAGE HAS DELIBERATELY BEEN LEFT BLANK

Pupil's Full Name:

Instructions:
Mark the boxes correctly like this ▲

Please sign your name here:

Comprehension

Example 1

A · B · C · D · E

Practice Question 1

A · B · C · D · E

	A	B	C	D	E
1	A	B	C	D	E
2	A	B	C	D	E
3	A	B	C	D	E
4	A	B	C	D	E
5	A	B	C	D	E
6	A	B	C	D	E
7	A	B	C	D	E
8	A	B	C	D	E
9	A	B	C	D	E
10	A	B	C	D	E

Shuffled Sentences

Example 1

A · B · C · D · E

Practice Question 1

A · B · C · D · E

	A	B	C	D	E
1	A	B	C	D	E
2	A	B	C	D	E
3	A	B	C	D	E
4	A	B	C	D	E
5	A	B	C	D	E
6	A	B	C	D	E
7	A	B	C	D	E
8	A	B	C	D	E
9	A	B	C	D	E
10	A	B	C	D	E
11	A	B	C	D	E
12	A	B	C	D	E
13	A	B	C	D	E
14	A	B	C	D	E
15	A	B	C	D	E

Numeracy

Example 1 — 3 7

Practice Question 1

1

2

3

4

5

6

7

8

9

10

11

12

13

(Each answer box contains columns of digits 0–9.)

Problem Solving

Example 1

  Ⓐ Ⓑ Ⓒ Ⓓ Ⓔ

Practice Question 1

  Ⓐ Ⓑ Ⓒ Ⓓ Ⓔ

	A	B	C	D	E
1	Ⓐ	Ⓑ	Ⓒ	Ⓓ	Ⓔ
2	Ⓐ	Ⓑ	Ⓒ	Ⓓ	Ⓔ
3	Ⓐ	Ⓑ	Ⓒ	Ⓓ	Ⓔ
4	Ⓐ	Ⓑ	Ⓒ	Ⓓ	Ⓔ
5	Ⓐ	Ⓑ	Ⓒ	Ⓓ	Ⓔ
6	Ⓐ	Ⓑ	Ⓒ	Ⓓ	Ⓔ
7	Ⓐ	Ⓑ	Ⓒ	Ⓓ	Ⓔ
8	Ⓐ	Ⓑ	Ⓒ	Ⓓ	Ⓔ
9	Ⓐ	Ⓑ	Ⓒ	Ⓓ	Ⓔ
10	Ⓐ	Ⓑ	Ⓒ	Ⓓ	Ⓔ

Synonyms

Example 1

  Ⓐ Ⓑ Ⓒ Ⓓ Ⓔ

Practice Question 1

  Ⓐ Ⓑ Ⓒ Ⓓ Ⓔ

	A	B	C	D	E
1	Ⓐ	Ⓑ	Ⓒ	Ⓓ	Ⓔ
2	Ⓐ	Ⓑ	Ⓒ	Ⓓ	Ⓔ
3	Ⓐ	Ⓑ	Ⓒ	Ⓓ	Ⓔ
4	Ⓐ	Ⓑ	Ⓒ	Ⓓ	Ⓔ
5	Ⓐ	Ⓑ	Ⓒ	Ⓓ	Ⓔ
6	Ⓐ	Ⓑ	Ⓒ	Ⓓ	Ⓔ
7	Ⓐ	Ⓑ	Ⓒ	Ⓓ	Ⓔ
8	Ⓐ	Ⓑ	Ⓒ	Ⓓ	Ⓔ
9	Ⓐ	Ⓑ	Ⓒ	Ⓓ	Ⓔ
10	Ⓐ	Ⓑ	Ⓒ	Ⓓ	Ⓔ
11	Ⓐ	Ⓑ	Ⓒ	Ⓓ	Ⓔ
12	Ⓐ	Ⓑ	Ⓒ	Ⓓ	Ⓔ
13	Ⓐ	Ⓑ	Ⓒ	Ⓓ	Ⓔ
14	Ⓐ	Ⓑ	Ⓒ	Ⓓ	Ⓔ
15	Ⓐ	Ⓑ	Ⓒ	Ⓓ	Ⓔ
16	Ⓐ	Ⓑ	Ⓒ	Ⓓ	Ⓔ
17	Ⓐ	Ⓑ	Ⓒ	Ⓓ	Ⓔ
18	Ⓐ	Ⓑ	Ⓒ	Ⓓ	Ⓔ
19	Ⓐ	Ⓑ	Ⓒ	Ⓓ	Ⓔ
20	Ⓐ	Ⓑ	Ⓒ	Ⓓ	Ⓔ
21	Ⓐ	Ⓑ	Ⓒ	Ⓓ	Ⓔ

	A	B	C	D	E
22	Ⓐ	Ⓑ	Ⓒ	Ⓓ	Ⓔ
23	Ⓐ	Ⓑ	Ⓒ	Ⓓ	Ⓔ
24	Ⓐ	Ⓑ	Ⓒ	Ⓓ	Ⓔ

Non-Verbal Reasoning

COMPLETE THE SEQUENCE
Example 1

  Ⓐ Ⓑ Ⓒ Ⓓ Ⓔ

COMPLETE THE SEQUENCE
Practice Question 1

  Ⓐ Ⓑ Ⓒ Ⓓ Ⓔ

COMPLETE THE SQUARE Example 2

  Ⓐ Ⓑ Ⓒ Ⓓ Ⓔ

COMPLETE THE SQUARE
Practice Question 2

  Ⓐ Ⓑ Ⓒ Ⓓ Ⓔ

	A	B	C	D	E
1	Ⓐ	Ⓑ	Ⓒ	Ⓓ	Ⓔ
2	Ⓐ	Ⓑ	Ⓒ	Ⓓ	Ⓔ
3	Ⓐ	Ⓑ	Ⓒ	Ⓓ	Ⓔ
4	Ⓐ	Ⓑ	Ⓒ	Ⓓ	Ⓔ
5	Ⓐ	Ⓑ	Ⓒ	Ⓓ	Ⓔ
6	Ⓐ	Ⓑ	Ⓒ	Ⓓ	Ⓔ
7	Ⓐ	Ⓑ	Ⓒ	Ⓓ	Ⓔ
8	Ⓐ	Ⓑ	Ⓒ	Ⓓ	Ⓔ
9	Ⓐ	Ⓑ	Ⓒ	Ⓓ	Ⓔ
10	Ⓐ	Ⓑ	Ⓒ	Ⓓ	Ⓔ
11	Ⓐ	Ⓑ	Ⓒ	Ⓓ	Ⓔ
12	Ⓐ	Ⓑ	Ⓒ	Ⓓ	Ⓔ
13	Ⓐ	Ⓑ	Ⓒ	Ⓓ	Ⓔ

Pupil's Full Name:

Instructions:
Mark the boxes correctly like this ▲

Please sign your name here:

Problem Solving

Example 1

Ⓐ B C D E F G H I J

Practice Question 1

A B C D E F G H I J

1 A B C D E F G H I J
2 A B C D E F G H I J
3 A B C D E F G H I J
4 A B C D E F G H I J
5 A B C D E F G H I J
6 A B C D E F G H I J
7 A B C D E F G H I J
8 A B C D E F G H I J
9 A B C D E F G H I J
10 A B C D E F G H I J

Cloze

Example 1

Ⓐ B C D E

Practice Question 1

A B C D E

1 A B C D E F G H I J
2 A B C D E F G H I J
3 A B C D E F G H I J
4 A B C D E F G H I J
5 A B C D E F G H I J
6 A B C D E F G H I J
7 A B C D E F G H I J
8 A B C D E F G H I J
9 A B C D E F G H I J
10 A B C D E F G H I J
11 A B C D E F G H I J
12 A B C D E F G H I J
13 A B C D E F G H I J
14 A B C D E F G H I J

15 A B C D E F G H I J
16 A B C D E F G H I J
17 A B C D E F G H I J
18 A B C D E F G H I J
19 A B C D E F G H I J
20 A B C D E F G H I J

Non-Verbal Reasoning

ROTATION Example 1

A B C D E

ROTATION Practice Question 1

A B C D E

CODES Example 2

A B C D E

CODES Practice Question 2

A B C D E

1 A B C D E
2 A B C D E
3 A B C D E
4 A B C D E
5 A B C D E
6 A B C D E
7 A B C D E
8 A B C D E
9 A B C D E
10 A B C D E
11 A B C D E
12 A B C D E
13 A B C D E
14 A B C D E
15 A B C D E

Grammar

Example 1

	A	B	C	D	E
	A	B	~~C~~	D	E

Practice Question 1

	A	B	C	D	E
	A	B	C	D	E
1	A	B	C	D	E
2	A	B	C	D	E
3	A	B	C	D	E
4	A	B	C	D	E
5	A	B	C	D	E
6	A	B	C	D	E
7	A	B	C	D	E
8	A	B	C	D	E

Antonyms

Example 1

	A	B	C	D	E
	~~A~~	B	C	D	E

Practice Question 1

	A	B	C	D	E
	A	B	C	D	E
1	A	B	C	D	E
2	A	B	C	D	E
3	A	B	C	D	E
4	A	B	C	D	E
5	A	B	C	D	E
6	A	B	C	D	E
7	A	B	C	D	E
8	A	B	C	D	E
9	A	B	C	D	E
10	A	B	C	D	E
11	A	B	C	D	E
12	A	B	C	D	E
13	A	B	C	D	E
14	A	B	C	D	E
15	A	B	C	D	E

Numeracy

Example 1

3 7

Practice Question 1   1   2

(Number grids 0–9 for Example 1, Practice Question 1, 1, 2)

3   4   5   6

(Number grids 0–9)

7   8

(Number grids 0–9)

	A	B	C	D	E
9	A	B	C	D	E
10	A	B	C	D	E
11	A	B	C	D	E
12	A	B	C	D	E
13	A	B	C	D	E
14	A	B	C	D	E
15	A	B	C	D	E
16	A	B	C	D	E
17	A	B	C	D	E
18	A	B	C	D	E

Pupil's Full Name:

Instructions:
Mark the boxes correctly like this ▬

Please sign your name here:

Comprehension

Example 1

	A	B	C	D	E

Practice Question 1

	A	B	C	D	E
1	A	B	C	D	E
2	A	B	C	D	E
3	A	B	C	D	E
4	A	B	C	D	E
5	A	B	C	D	E
6	A	B	C	D	E
7	A	B	C	D	E
8	A	B	C	D	E
9	A	B	C	D	E
10	A	B	C	D	E

Shuffled Sentences

Example 1

	A	B	C	D	E

Practice Question 1

	A	B	C	D	E
1	A	B	C	D	E
2	A	B	C	D	E
3	A	B	C	D	E
4	A	B	C	D	E
5	A	B	C	D	E
6	A	B	C	D	E
7	A	B	C	D	E
8	A	B	C	D	E
9	A	B	C	D	E
10	A	B	C	D	E
11	A	B	C	D	E
12	A	B	C	D	E
13	A	B	C	D	E
14	A	B	C	D	E
15	A	B	C	D	E

Numeracy

Example 1

3 7

Practice Question 1

1

2

3

4

5

6

7

8

9

10

11

12

13

(Answer grids with digits 0–9 for each question)

Problem Solving

Example 1

~~A~~ B̶ C̶ D̶ E̶ F̶ G̶ H̶ I̶ J̶

Practice Question 1

A̶ B̶ C̶ D̶ E̶ F̶ G̶ H̶ I̶ J̶

1	A̶	B̶	C̶	D̶	E̶	F̶	G̶	H̶	I̶	J̶
2	A̶	B̶	C̶	D̶	E̶	F̶	G̶	H̶	I̶	J̶
3	A̶	B̶	C̶	D̶	E̶	F̶	G̶	H̶	I̶	J̶
4	A̶	B̶	C̶	D̶	E̶	F̶	G̶	H̶	I̶	J̶
5	A̶	B̶	C̶	D̶	E̶	F̶	G̶	H̶	I̶	J̶
6	A̶	B̶	C̶	D̶	E̶	F̶	G̶	H̶	I̶	J̶
7	A̶	B̶	C̶	D̶	E̶	F̶	G̶	H̶	I̶	J̶
8	A̶	B̶	C̶	D̶	E̶	F̶	G̶	H̶	I̶	J̶
9	A̶	B̶	C̶	D̶	E̶	F̶	G̶	H̶	I̶	J̶
10	A̶	B̶	C̶	D̶	E̶	F̶	G̶	H̶	I̶	J̶

Synonyms

Example 1

A̶ B̶ C̶ D̶ ~~E~~

Practice Question 1

A̶ B̶ C̶ D̶ E̶

1	A̶	B̶	C̶	D̶	E̶
2	A̶	B̶	C̶	D̶	E̶
3	A̶	B̶	C̶	D̶	E̶
4	A̶	B̶	C̶	D̶	E̶
5	A̶	B̶	C̶	D̶	E̶
6	A̶	B̶	C̶	D̶	E̶
7	A̶	B̶	C̶	D̶	E̶
8	A̶	B̶	C̶	D̶	E̶
9	A̶	B̶	C̶	D̶	E̶
10	A̶	B̶	C̶	D̶	E̶
11	A̶	B̶	C̶	D̶	E̶
12	A̶	B̶	C̶	D̶	E̶
13	A̶	B̶	C̶	D̶	E̶
14	A̶	B̶	C̶	D̶	E̶
15	A̶	B̶	C̶	D̶	E̶
16	A̶	B̶	C̶	D̶	E̶
17	A̶	B̶	C̶	D̶	E̶
18	A̶	B̶	C̶	D̶	E̶
19	A̶	B̶	C̶	D̶	E̶
20	A̶	B̶	C̶	D̶	E̶
21	A̶	B̶	C̶	D̶	E̶

22	A̶	B̶	C̶	D̶	E̶
23	A̶	B̶	C̶	D̶	E̶

Non-Verbal Reasoning

COMPLETE THE SEQUENCE
Example 1

A̶ B̶ ~~C~~ D̶ E̶

COMPLETE THE SEQUENCE
Practice Question 1

A̶ B̶ C̶ D̶ E̶

1	A̶	B̶	C̶	D̶	E̶
2	A̶	B̶	C̶	D̶	E̶
3	A̶	B̶	C̶	D̶	E̶
4	A̶	B̶	C̶	D̶	E̶
5	A̶	B̶	C̶	D̶	E̶
6	A̶	B̶	C̶	D̶	E̶
7	A̶	B̶	C̶	D̶	E̶
8	A̶	B̶	C̶	D̶	E̶
9	A̶	B̶	C̶	D̶	E̶
10	A̶	B̶	C̶	D̶	E̶
11	A̶	B̶	C̶	D̶	E̶
12	A̶	B̶	C̶	D̶	E̶
13	A̶	B̶	C̶	D̶	E̶
14	A̶	B̶	C̶	D̶	E̶

Pupil's Full Name:

Instructions:
Mark the boxes correctly like this ▲

Please sign your name here:

Problem Solving

Example 1

Ⓐ B C D E F G H ⊢ ⊣

Practice Question 1

A B C D E F G H ⊢ ⊣

1 A B C D E F G H ⊢ ⊣
2 A B C D E F G H ⊢ ⊣
3 A B C D E F G H ⊢ ⊣
4 A B C D E F G H ⊢ ⊣
5 A B C D E F G H ⊢ ⊣
6 A B C D E F G H ⊢ ⊣
7 A B C D E F G H ⊢ ⊣
8 A B C D E F G H ⊢ ⊣
9 A B C D E F G H ⊢ ⊣
10 A B C D E F G H ⊢ ⊣

Cloze

Example 1

Ⓐ B C D E

Practice Question 1

A B C D E

1 A B C D E F G H ⊢ ⊣
2 A B C D E F G H ⊢ ⊣
3 A B C D E F G H ⊢ ⊣
4 A B C D E F G H ⊢ ⊣
5 A B C D E F G H ⊢ ⊣
6 A B C D E F G H ⊢ ⊣
7 A B C D E F G H ⊢ ⊣
8 A B C D E F G H ⊢ ⊣
9 A B C D E F G H ⊢ ⊣
10 A B C D E F G H ⊢ ⊣
11 A B C D E F G H ⊢ ⊣
12 A B C D E F G H ⊢ ⊣
13 A B C D E F G H ⊢ ⊣
14 A B C D E F G H ⊢ ⊣

15 A B C D E F G H ⊢ ⊣
16 A B C D E F G H ⊢ ⊣
17 A B C D E F G H ⊢ ⊣
18 A B C D E F G H ⊢ ⊣
19 A B C D E F G H ⊢ ⊣
20 A B C D E F G H ⊢ ⊣

Non-Verbal Reasoning

CUBE NET Example 1

A B C D Ⓔ

CUBE NET Practice Question 1

A B C D E

LEAST SIMILAR Example 2

A Ⓑ C D E

LEAST SIMILAR Practice Question 2

A B C D E

1 A B C D E
2 A B C D E
3 A B C D E
4 A B C D E
5 A B C D E
6 A B C D E
7 A B C D E
8 A B C D E
9 A B C D E
10 A B C D E
11 A B C D E
12 A B C D E
13 A B C D E

Antonyms

Example 1

   A   B   C   D   E

Practice Question 1

   A   B   C   D   E

1   A   B   C   D   E
2   A   B   C   D   E
3   A   B   C   D   E
4   A   B   C   D   E
5   A   B   C   D   E
6   A   B   C   D   E
7   A   B   C   D   E
8   A   B   C   D   E
9   A   B   C   D   E
10   A   B   C   D   E
11   A   B   C   D   E
12   A   B   C   D   E
13   A   B   C   D   E
14   A   B   C   D   E
15   A   B   C   D   E

Numeracy

Example 1

3 7

Practice Question 1

1

2

3

4

5

6

7 **8** **9** **10**

11 **12** **13** **14**

15 **16** **17** **18**

Pupil's Full Name:

Instructions:
Mark the boxes correctly like this ◆

Please sign your name here:

Comprehension

Example 1

| Ⓐ | Ⓑ | Ⓒ | Ⓓ | Ⓔ |

Practice Question 1

| Ⓐ | Ⓑ | Ⓒ | Ⓓ | Ⓔ |

	A	B	C	D	E
1	Ⓐ	Ⓑ	Ⓒ	Ⓓ	Ⓔ
2	Ⓐ	Ⓑ	Ⓒ	Ⓓ	Ⓔ
3	Ⓐ	Ⓑ	Ⓒ	Ⓓ	Ⓔ
4	Ⓐ	Ⓑ	Ⓒ	Ⓓ	Ⓔ
5	Ⓐ	Ⓑ	Ⓒ	Ⓓ	Ⓔ
6	Ⓐ	Ⓑ	Ⓒ	Ⓓ	Ⓔ
7	Ⓐ	Ⓑ	Ⓒ	Ⓓ	Ⓔ
8	Ⓐ	Ⓑ	Ⓒ	Ⓓ	Ⓔ
9	Ⓐ	Ⓑ	Ⓒ	Ⓓ	Ⓔ
10	Ⓐ	Ⓑ	Ⓒ	Ⓓ	Ⓔ

Grammar

Example 1

| Ⓐ | Ⓑ | Ⓒ | Ⓓ | Ⓔ |

Practice Question 1

| Ⓐ | Ⓑ | Ⓒ | Ⓓ | Ⓔ |

	A	B	C	D	E
1	Ⓐ	Ⓑ	Ⓒ	Ⓓ	Ⓔ
2	Ⓐ	Ⓑ	Ⓒ	Ⓓ	Ⓔ
3	Ⓐ	Ⓑ	Ⓒ	Ⓓ	Ⓔ
4	Ⓐ	Ⓑ	Ⓒ	Ⓓ	Ⓔ
5	Ⓐ	Ⓑ	Ⓒ	Ⓓ	Ⓔ
6	Ⓐ	Ⓑ	Ⓒ	Ⓓ	Ⓔ
7	Ⓐ	Ⓑ	Ⓒ	Ⓓ	Ⓔ
8	Ⓐ	Ⓑ	Ⓒ	Ⓓ	Ⓔ
9	Ⓐ	Ⓑ	Ⓒ	Ⓓ	Ⓔ

Numeracy

Example 1

| Ⓐ | Ⓑ | Ⓒ | Ⓓ | Ⓔ |

Practice Question 1

| Ⓐ | Ⓑ | Ⓒ | Ⓓ | Ⓔ |

	A	B	C	D	E
1	Ⓐ	Ⓑ	Ⓒ	Ⓓ	Ⓔ
2	Ⓐ	Ⓑ	Ⓒ	Ⓓ	Ⓔ
3	Ⓐ	Ⓑ	Ⓒ	Ⓓ	Ⓔ
4	Ⓐ	Ⓑ	Ⓒ	Ⓓ	Ⓔ
5	Ⓐ	Ⓑ	Ⓒ	Ⓓ	Ⓔ
6	Ⓐ	Ⓑ	Ⓒ	Ⓓ	Ⓔ
7	Ⓐ	Ⓑ	Ⓒ	Ⓓ	Ⓔ
8	Ⓐ	Ⓑ	Ⓒ	Ⓓ	Ⓔ
9	Ⓐ	Ⓑ	Ⓒ	Ⓓ	Ⓔ
10	Ⓐ	Ⓑ	Ⓒ	Ⓓ	Ⓔ
11	Ⓐ	Ⓑ	Ⓒ	Ⓓ	Ⓔ
12	Ⓐ	Ⓑ	Ⓒ	Ⓓ	Ⓔ
13	Ⓐ	Ⓑ	Ⓒ	Ⓓ	Ⓔ
14	Ⓐ	Ⓑ	Ⓒ	Ⓓ	Ⓔ
15	Ⓐ	Ⓑ	Ⓒ	Ⓓ	Ⓔ
16	Ⓐ	Ⓑ	Ⓒ	Ⓓ	Ⓔ
17	Ⓐ	Ⓑ	Ⓒ	Ⓓ	Ⓔ
18	Ⓐ	Ⓑ	Ⓒ	Ⓓ	Ⓔ
19	Ⓐ	Ⓑ	Ⓒ	Ⓓ	Ⓔ
20	Ⓐ	Ⓑ	Ⓒ	Ⓓ	Ⓔ
21	Ⓐ	Ⓑ	Ⓒ	Ⓓ	Ⓔ
22	Ⓐ	Ⓑ	Ⓒ	Ⓓ	Ⓔ
23	Ⓐ	Ⓑ	Ⓒ	Ⓓ	Ⓔ
24	Ⓐ	Ⓑ	Ⓒ	Ⓓ	Ⓔ
25	Ⓐ	Ⓑ	Ⓒ	Ⓓ	Ⓔ
26	Ⓐ	Ⓑ	Ⓒ	Ⓓ	Ⓔ
27	Ⓐ	Ⓑ	Ⓒ	Ⓓ	Ⓔ
28	Ⓐ	Ⓑ	Ⓒ	Ⓓ	Ⓔ
29	Ⓐ	Ⓑ	Ⓒ	Ⓓ	Ⓔ
30	Ⓐ	Ⓑ	Ⓒ	Ⓓ	Ⓔ
31	Ⓐ	Ⓑ	Ⓒ	Ⓓ	Ⓔ
32	Ⓐ	Ⓑ	Ⓒ	Ⓓ	Ⓔ

33	A	B	C	D	E
34	A	B	C	D	E
35	A	B	C	D	E
36	A	B	C	D	E
37	A	B	C	D	E
38	A	B	C	D	E
39	A	B	C	D	E

Synonyms

Example 1

	A	B	C	D	E

Practice Question 1

	A	B	C	D	E
1	A	B	C	D	E
2	A	B	C	D	E
3	A	B	C	D	E
4	A	B	C	D	E
5	A	B	C	D	E
6	A	B	C	D	E
7	A	B	C	D	E
8	A	B	C	D	E
9	A	B	C	D	E
10	A	B	C	D	E
11	A	B	C	D	E
12	A	B	C	D	E
13	A	B	C	D	E
14	A	B	C	D	E
15	A	B	C	D	E
16	A	B	C	D	E
17	A	B	C	D	E
18	A	B	C	D	E
19	A	B	C	D	E
20	A	B	C	D	E

Non-Verbal Reasoning

ROTATION Example 1

A	B	C	D	E

ROTATION Practice Question 1

A	B	C	D	E

COMPLETE THE SQUARE Example 2

A	B	C	D	E

COMPLETE THE SQUARE
Practice Question 2

	A	B	C	D	E
1	A	B	C	D	E
2	A	B	C	D	E
3	A	B	C	D	E
4	A	B	C	D	E
5	A	B	C	D	E
6	A	B	C	D	E
7	A	B	C	D	E
8	A	B	C	D	E
9	A	B	C	D	E
10	A	B	C	D	E
11	A	B	C	D	E
12	A	B	C	D	E
13	A	B	C	D	E

Pupil's Full Name:

2

Instructions:
Mark the boxes correctly like this ⬆A

Please sign your name here:

Cloze Sentences

Example 1

Ⓐ   Ⓑ   Ⓒ   ~~Ⓓ~~   Ⓔ

Practice Question 1

Ⓐ   Ⓑ   Ⓒ   Ⓓ   Ⓔ

Example 2   _____ten_____

Practice Question 2   _____

1	Ⓐ	Ⓑ	Ⓒ	Ⓓ	Ⓔ
2	Ⓐ	Ⓑ	Ⓒ	Ⓓ	Ⓔ
3	Ⓐ	Ⓑ	Ⓒ	Ⓓ	Ⓔ
4	Ⓐ	Ⓑ	Ⓒ	Ⓓ	Ⓔ
5	Ⓐ	Ⓑ	Ⓒ	Ⓓ	Ⓔ
6	Ⓐ	Ⓑ	Ⓒ	Ⓓ	Ⓔ
7	Ⓐ	Ⓑ	Ⓒ	Ⓓ	Ⓔ
8	Ⓐ	Ⓑ	Ⓒ	Ⓓ	Ⓔ
9	Ⓐ	Ⓑ	Ⓒ	Ⓓ	Ⓔ
10	Ⓐ	Ⓑ	Ⓒ	Ⓓ	Ⓔ

11 _____
12 _____
13 _____
14 _____
15 _____
16 _____
17 _____

Problem Solving

Example 1

⬆Ⓐ Ⓑ Ⓒ Ⓓ Ⓔ Ⓕ Ⓖ Ⓗ Ⓘ Ⓙ

Practice Question 1

Ⓐ Ⓑ Ⓒ Ⓓ Ⓔ Ⓕ Ⓖ Ⓗ Ⓘ Ⓙ

1	Ⓐ	Ⓑ	Ⓒ	Ⓓ	Ⓔ	Ⓕ	Ⓖ	Ⓗ	Ⓘ	Ⓙ
2	Ⓐ	Ⓑ	Ⓒ	Ⓓ	Ⓔ	Ⓕ	Ⓖ	Ⓗ	Ⓘ	Ⓙ
3	Ⓐ	Ⓑ	Ⓒ	Ⓓ	Ⓔ	Ⓕ	Ⓖ	Ⓗ	Ⓘ	Ⓙ
4	Ⓐ	Ⓑ	Ⓒ	Ⓓ	Ⓔ	Ⓕ	Ⓖ	Ⓗ	Ⓘ	Ⓙ
5	Ⓐ	Ⓑ	Ⓒ	Ⓓ	Ⓔ	Ⓕ	Ⓖ	Ⓗ	Ⓘ	Ⓙ
6	Ⓐ	Ⓑ	Ⓒ	Ⓓ	Ⓔ	Ⓕ	Ⓖ	Ⓗ	Ⓘ	Ⓙ
7	Ⓐ	Ⓑ	Ⓒ	Ⓓ	Ⓔ	Ⓕ	Ⓖ	Ⓗ	Ⓘ	Ⓙ
8	Ⓐ	Ⓑ	Ⓒ	Ⓓ	Ⓔ	Ⓕ	Ⓖ	Ⓗ	Ⓘ	Ⓙ
9	Ⓐ	Ⓑ	Ⓒ	Ⓓ	Ⓔ	Ⓕ	Ⓖ	Ⓗ	Ⓘ	Ⓙ
10	Ⓐ	Ⓑ	Ⓒ	Ⓓ	Ⓔ	Ⓕ	Ⓖ	Ⓗ	Ⓘ	Ⓙ

Antonyms

Example 1

	A	B	C	D	E
	A	B	C	D	E

Practice Question 1

	A	B	C	D	E
1	A	B	C	D	E
2	A	B	C	D	E
3	A	B	C	D	E
4	A	B	C	D	E
5	A	B	C	D	E
6	A	B	C	D	E
7	A	B	C	D	E
8	A	B	C	D	E
9	A	B	C	D	E
10	A	B	C	D	E
11	A	B	C	D	E
12	A	B	C	D	E
13	A	B	C	D	E
14	A	B	C	D	E
15	A	B	C	D	E
16	A	B	C	D	E
17	A	B	C	D	E
18	A	B	C	D	E
19	A	B	C	D	E
20	A	B	C	D	E
21	A	B	C	D	E
22	A	B	C	D	E
23	A	B	C	D	E
24	A	B	C	D	E
25	A	B	C	D	E

Non-Verbal Reasoning

COMPLETE THE SQUARE Example 1

A	B	C	D	E
A	B	C	D	E

COMPLETE THE SQUARE Practice Question 1

A	B	C	D	E
A	B	C	D	E

REFLECTION Example 2

A	B	C	D	E
A	B	C	D	E

REFLECTION Practice Question 2

	A	B	C	D	E
1	A	B	C	D	E
2	A	B	C	D	E

3	A	B	C	D	E
4	A	B	C	D	E
5	A	B	C	D	E
6	A	B	C	D	E
7	A	B	C	D	E
8	A	B	C	D	E
9	A	B	C	D	E
10	A	B	C	D	E
11	A	B	C	D	E
12	A	B	C	D	E
13	A	B	C	D	E
14	A	B	C	D	E
15	A	B	C	D	E

Shuffled Sentences

Example 1

	A	B	C	D	E
	A	B	C	D	E

Practice Question 1

	A	B	C	D	E
1	A	B	C	D	E
2	A	B	C	D	E
3	A	B	C	D	E
4	A	B	C	D	E
5	A	B	C	D	E
6	A	B	C	D	E
7	A	B	C	D	E
8	A	B	C	D	E
9	A	B	C	D	E
10	A	B	C	D	E
11	A	B	C	D	E
12	A	B	C	D	E
13	A	B	C	D	E
14	A	B	C	D	E
15	A	B	C	D	E

Pupil's Full Name:

Instructions:
Mark the boxes correctly like this ⬥

Please sign your name here:

Comprehension

Example 1

A B C D E

Practice Question 1

A B C D E

	A	B	C	D	E
1	A	B	C	D	E
2	A	B	C	D	E
3	A	B	C	D	E
4	A	B	C	D	E
5	A	B	C	D	E
6	A	B	C	D	E
7	A	B	C	D	E
8	A	B	C	D	E
9	A	B	C	D	E
10	A	B	C	D	E
11	A	B	C	D	E
12	A	B	C	D	E
13	A	B	C	D	E
14	A	B	C	D	E

	A	B	C	D	E
11	A	B	C	D	E
12	A	B	C	D	E
13	A	B	C	D	E
14	A	B	C	D	E
15	A	B	C	D	E
16	A	B	C	D	E
17	A	B	C	D	E
18	A	B	C	D	E
19	A	B	C	D	E
20	A	B	C	D	E
21	A	B	C	D	E
22	A	B	C	D	E
23	A	B	C	D	E
24	A	B	C	D	E
25	A	B	C	D	E
26	A	B	C	D	E
27	A	B	C	D	E
28	A	B	C	D	E

Numeracy

Example 1

A B C D E

Practice Question 1

A B C D E

	A	B	C	D	E
1	A	B	C	D	E
2	A	B	C	D	E
3	A	B	C	D	E
4	A	B	C	D	E
5	A	B	C	D	E
6	A	B	C	D	E
7	A	B	C	D	E
8	A	B	C	D	E
9	A	B	C	D	E
10	A	B	C	D	E

Synonyms

Example 1

	A	B	C	D	E

Practice Question 1

	A	B	C	D	E
1	A	B	C	D	E
2	A	B	C	D	E
3	A	B	C	D	E
4	A	B	C	D	E
5	A	B	C	D	E
6	A	B	C	D	E
7	A	B	C	D	E
8	A	B	C	D	E
9	A	B	C	D	E
10	A	B	C	D	E
11	A	B	C	D	E
12	A	B	C	D	E
13	A	B	C	D	E
14	A	B	C	D	E
15	A	B	C	D	E
16	A	B	C	D	E
17	A	B	C	D	E
18	A	B	C	D	E
19	A	B	C	D	E
20	A	B	C	D	E

Non-Verbal Reasoning

REFLECTION Example 1

	A	B	C	D	E

REFLECTION Practice Question 1

	A	B	C	D	E

ROTATION Example 2

	A	B	C	D	E

ROTATION Practice Question 2

	A	B	C	D	E

LEAST SIMILAR Example 3

	A	B	C	D	E

LEAST SIMILAR Practice Question 3

	A	B	C	D	E
1	A	B	C	D	E
2	A	B	C	D	E
3	A	B	C	D	E
4	A	B	C	D	E
5	A	B	C	D	E
6	A	B	C	D	E
7	A	B	C	D	E
8	A	B	C	D	E
9	A	B	C	D	E
10	A	B	C	D	E
11	A	B	C	D	E
12	A	B	C	D	E
13	A	B	C	D	E
14	A	B	C	D	E
15	A	B	C	D	E

Pupil's Full Name:

Instructions:
Mark the boxes correctly like this ▲

Please sign your name here:

Cloze Sentences

Example 1

Ⓐ B C D E F G H ┼ ┤

Practice Question 1

A B C D E F G H ┼ ┤

Example 2 _____ ten _____

Practice Question 2 _____

1	A B C D E F G H ┼ ┤
2	A B C D E F G H ┼ ┤
3	A B C D E F G H ┼ ┤
4	A B C D E F G H ┼ ┤
5	A B C D E F G H ┼ ┤
6	A B C D E F G H ┼ ┤
7	A B C D E F G H ┼ ┤
8	A B C D E F G H ┼ ┤
9	A B C D E F G H ┼ ┤
10	A B C D E F G H ┼ ┤
11	_____
12	_____
13	_____
14	_____
15	_____
16	_____
17	_____

Problem Solving

Example 1

Ⓐ B C D E F G H ┼ ┤

Practice Question 1

A B C D E F G H ┼ ┤

1	A B C D E F G H ┼ ┤
2	A B C D E F G H ┼ ┤
3	A B C D E F G H ┼ ┤
4	A B C D E F G H ┼ ┤
5	A B C D E F G H ┼ ┤
6	A B C D E F G H ┼ ┤
7	A B C D E F G H ┼ ┤
8	A B C D E F G H ┼ ┤
9	A B C D E F G H ┼ ┤
10	A B C D E F G H ┼ ┤

Antonyms

Example 1

A	B	C	D	E

Practice Question 1

	A	B	C	D	E
1	A	B	C	D	E
2	A	B	C	D	E
3	A	B	C	D	E
4	A	B	C	D	E
5	A	B	C	D	E
6	A	B	C	D	E
7	A	B	C	D	E
8	A	B	C	D	E
9	A	B	C	D	E
10	A	B	C	D	E
11	A	B	C	D	E
12	A	B	C	D	E
13	A	B	C	D	E
14	A	B	C	D	E
15	A	B	C	D	E
16	A	B	C	D	E
17	A	B	C	D	E
18	A	B	C	D	E
19	A	B	C	D	E
20	A	B	C	D	E
21	A	B	C	D	E
22	A	B	C	D	E
23	A	B	C	D	E
24	A	B	C	D	E
25	A	B	C	D	E

Non-Verbal Reasoning

CUBES Example 1

A	B	C	D	E

CUBES Practice Question 1

A	B	C	D	E

REFLECTION Example 2

A	B	C	D	E

REFLECTION Practice Question 2

A	B	C	D	E

CODES Example 3

A	B	C	D	E

CODES Practice Question 3

	A	B	C	D	E
1	A	B	C	D	E
2	A	B	C	D	E
3	A	B	C	D	E
4	A	B	C	D	E
5	A	B	C	D	E
6	A	B	C	D	E
7	A	B	C	D	E
8	A	B	C	D	E
9	A	B	C	D	E
10	A	B	C	D	E
11	A	B	C	D	E
12	A	B	C	D	E
13	A	B	C	D	E
14	A	B	C	D	E
15	A	B	C	D	E

Shuffled Sentences

Example 1

A	B	C	D	E

Practice Question 1

	A	B	C	D	E
1	A	B	C	D	E
2	A	B	C	D	E
3	A	B	C	D	E
4	A	B	C	D	E
5	A	B	C	D	E
6	A	B	C	D	E
7	A	B	C	D	E
8	A	B	C	D	E
9	A	B	C	D	E
10	A	B	C	D	E
11	A	B	C	D	E
12	A	B	C	D	E
13	A	B	C	D	E
14	A	B	C	D	E
15	A	B	C	D	E